Raising Godly Kids

52 Guidelines for
Counter-Culture Parenting

Harold J. Sala

CAMP HILL, PENNSYLVANIA

Christian Publications, Inc.
3825 Hartzdale Drive
Camp Hill, PA 17011
www.cpi-horizon.com
www.christianpublications.com

Faithful, biblical publishing since 1883

Raising Godly Kids:
52 Guidelines for Counter-Culture Parenting
ISBN: 0-87509-927-0

LOC Control Number: 2001-130448

© 2001 by Christian Publications

Contents

Preface

Of all the people in the world, there is no exact replica (even a twin) of the child you bring into the world. Your baby is one of a kind. At conception 500 million sperm competed with each other to fertilize the ovum. Twenty-three chromosomes from you and the same number from your mate combined to give your child unique features of heredity from both sides of the family, reaching back for generations.

Apart from spiritual rebirth, nothing is more awesome than this marvelous phenomenon of reproducing yourselves in this little seven- or eight-pound bundle of life. A baby is God's gift of life. But it is merely the loan of a life. You don't own your child; you simply have eighteen years to pack his suitcase before he embarks on life's journey.

But once you have become a parent, it becomes apparent that your life will never be the same! Looking at that tiny bundle of joy in the hospital, no first-time parent has any concept—not even in his wildest imagination—of how his world is about to change forever. We soon learn that it's easy to be a parent—at least for most of us—but difficult to be a really good one!

Parenting is one of the most awesome and demanding tasks of life with its challenges, ups and downs, surprises, tears and joys. With recent changes in our world and our culture (how do you tell your children that immorality and dishonesty are wrong when national leaders admit to both?), the responsibility of raising moral, God-fearing children in a world that flaunts Christian values, often ignores civility and decency, and laughs at traditional values becomes more difficult year by year—but certainly not impossible! God is still in the business of helping parents who are committed to Him, asking His help and following the guidelines of Scripture.

I feel for couples who—for whatever reason—are unable to have children, but I pity couples who as an act of their will choose *not* to have children, thus being deprived of the experience of seeing the growth, laughter, smiles, tears, the bumps and certainly the joy of a child growing to eventual maturity.

The selections in this book are not definitive—not a manual on how to do it, but guidelines and insights that will help you be a better parent. They often certify the obvious, which, at times, becomes obscured with the weariness, the stress and the busyness of life today. As you read these practical selections you will be reminded that you are the value system your youngster will adopt. Values are caught more than taught! I hope you will take time to ponder the insights at the end of each chapter and apply the applications to your parenting experiences.

There are no second chances with parenting! When you blow it, you can't go back and start over. You live with the consequences. You have no learning curve when you bring a baby home from the hospital, but you are embarking on what can be one of the most satisfying experiences of your life. I know, because we have raised three who are now raising their children very much as they were raised. And if I live long enough to see our grandchildren do the same thing, only then will I feel that I have really succeeded in this business of parenting.

Having been involved with families as a counselor, lecturer, family conference speaker and Bible teacher for more than four decades, I admit that with each passing year it becomes more challenging for godly parents to confront the culture of an ungodly world and raise kids so strong they won't need you when you are not there. You as a parent quickly learn that there will always be a tension between Christian values and the world in which your child grows up, and knowing how to react (but not overreact) when necessary and also act in love and compassion requires the skill of a diamond cutter and the balance of a tightrope walker. But with God's help you can do what needs to be done. *You can raise godly children in an ungodly world!*

Withdrawing from our world is not an option. Confronting the culture and raising your children to know and love the Lord is not only your responsibility before God, but can also be your greatest joy in life and your most important ministry and most lasting and significant accomplishment.

Children are God's way of saying, "Life must go on, and I want your children to walk with Me and to learn that I am sufficient to meet them, just as I met you a generation ago!"

I recommend that you read one selection each day, looking up the coordinated resource passages, meditating on what you read and striving to apply it to your child.

Be encouraged, friend! You can make the difference in the life of your child!

Harold J. Sala
Mission Viejo, California

Acknowledgments

Apart from the input and assistance of many people, books as this would not be possible. My special thanks to Maynard Eyestone who originally proofed the selections which were written for *Guidelines—A Five-Minute Commentary*. Then as we rewrote and adapted these for this book, Luisa Ampil provided generous assistance in editing and printing.

I would also like to extend my gratitude to Susan Schlabach and Barbour Publishing for the use of three selections included in this book—"Growing a Kid So Strong He Won't Need You When You Aren't There," "Raising Positive Kids in a Negative World" and "Growing Kids God's Way"—which are from my devotional book *Tomorrow Starts Today*.

My thanks also goes to George McPeek and Marilynne and Neill Foster of Christian Publications for making this book possible.

Our Greatest Mission Field

*"Like arrows in the hands of a warrior
are sons born in one's youth." (Psalm 127:4)*

The world's greatest mission field is not the dark continent of Africa, nor is it the highlands of Papua New Guinea or the jungles of South America—as needy as those places are. Are you ready for this? The greatest mission field today is the hearts of our children. And today forces more sinister and frightening than jungle vipers and more devastating than medicine-resistant malaria are making bids for the hearts of our children.

Our children are both our greatest challenge and our greatest mission field. But here is the question: How do we respond to the evil forces that challenge them? Turn off the TV set? Give them the gift of yourself and strive to include them in your overloaded schedule? Yes, but even more.

For a long while we parents have depended on others to do what we alone can do. We expect schools, churches and organizations to convey values and provide an educational framework. We expect that our offspring will absorb whatever is necessary to succeed in life, and so we pay for it—tuition for education, music lessons, karate and sports. We also provide computers, TVs, eighteen-speed bicycles, basketballs and the latest digital audio equipment. But often neglected is the personal element of parental love and the deeper lessons of what life is all about, including the spiritual.

I've often said that values in life are caught—not taught. I still believe that, but I also believe that the gift of parental love—the strong kind that includes caring enough to be there and to provide discipline and guidance until a child is old enough to make good decisions—is the only thing that will get kids through the jungle out there.

> *One of the greatest gifts parents can give their child is to love each other.*

When a child knows that he is really loved and will be accepted regardless of what happens, it gives him a stability which makes it much easier to stand on his own two feet and dare to be different. A parent's goal should be growing a kid so strong that he won't need you, and that can only be done through patient guidance, discipline and love.

What is the gift of love? Simply put, it is the gift of yourself. No longer do kids worry much about the earth being incinerated by nuclear fission, nor do many children worry about having enough to eat—though some do. But a lot of children today worry about whether Mommy and Daddy will stay together. The fear of divorce has now become children's greatest fear. One of the greatest gifts parents can give their child is to love each other.

The note left on the teacher's desk read, "Dear Mrs. Smith, I need a hug. At the end of the day, would you please give me a hug? I know you'd rather be hugging your own children but I'm hurting. Love, Becky." Becky was an eleven-year-old girl, overweight and desperate for love. Her mother had divorced her husband because she wanted her independence. Becky's grandmother was raising her and did the best she could. But there is no one who can take the place of your mother or father.

Dr. Ross Campbell, a psychiatrist whose book *How to Really Love Your Children* has more than half a million copies in print, says that he has never treated an adolescent involved in sexual misconduct who felt loved by his parents. Especially important is the love of a dad. Interestingly enough, the first mention of the word love in the Bible is that of a father's love for his son. The father was Abraham and the son was Isaac.

Insight

*O*ur first and greatest mission field is our children, and if we fail here, we register our greatest defeat.

Could Becky be your child, desperately in need of love? Remember, your child may be a mission field. Don't forget it.

Think on This

1. Realize that your children are not a hindrance to your "ministry." To the contrary, they *are* your ministry. Prioritize your time and energies appropriately.
2. Don't feel that time with your family—your children in particular—is wasted time that keeps you away from your business, your friends or whatever. Time spent with your

children is time building lives, growing godly kids in an ungodly world.

Resource Reading

Psalm 127

Love Starts at Home

*"Take your son, your only son, Isaac,
whom you love, and go. . . . Sacrifice him there
as a burnt offering." (Genesis 22:2)*

"What the world needs is love," goes the old song. It's still true, but it is not only the world—it's our families, and our children in particular. A study of the blueprint for family living found in the pages of the Bible will lead you to conclude that God intended the family to be a foretaste of heaven on earth, not a bit of hell on earth as it often is. His plan is for the family—your family—to be a miniature of the kingdom of God on earth, and what God expects of us in relationship to Himself, He expects of relationships in the family. God, who is love, puts a priority on love in our relationships.

The first mention of the word "love" in the Bible appears in the context of a family where God speaks of the love of a father toward his son. The father was Abraham, the progenitor of two great races of people, the Jews and the Arabs, and his son was Isaac. God said, "Take your son, your only son, Isaac, whom you love, and go. . . . Sacrifice him there as a burnt offering" (Genesis 22:2).

Remembering that Jesus stressed the importance of love in the family, keep in mind the fact that Jesus grew up in a normal family. Based on Matthew 13, following the birth of

Jesus, Mary and Joseph as husband and wife parented at least seven children. As the oldest brother in a family of at least eight, Jesus doubtless experienced all the frustrations of family living that put us under stress today.

> *Real love embraces sacrifice, not simply indulgence.*

Most family arguments start over trivial things—like who didn't clean up the mess in the kitchen or who squeezed the toothpaste in the middle. Why is it that love should often stop at the front door? Why should we feel that we can speak to each other at home in a tone that would cause our neighbors to punch our noses? Why is it that we often feel family members don't count when it comes to demonstrating and showing love—Christian love and commitment?

There is no questioning that Jesus taught love as the acid test of the fact God has touched a life with His presence. In the upper room, immediately before His ascension to heaven, Jesus said, "Love each other as I have loved you" (John 15:12). In the same message He said, "By this all men will know that you are my disciples, if you love one another" (13:35).

The definition of love that I like the best is that *love is an unconditional commitment to an imperfect individual to meet the needs of a person in such a manner that will require personal sacrifice.* Real love—the kind that holds our families together— is giving, not getting; it embraces sacrifice, not simply indulgence. This is not to suggest for a moment that in the beautiful relationship of marriage, love should not be expressed in the warmth and intimacy of sexual relations—it's right and normal, but love goes much beyond sex.

Love in the family is kept alive through little acts of kindness and thoughtfulness. The little kitchen motto, "Divine Service Performed Here Daily," has the right idea. Love is a commitment; it is a journey—not a destination—a way of life, a sacrament, a glue that holds families together. It is the answer to the sickness that has diseased our families and lives. It is what your children need more than toys, computers, music lessons, clothing fads and anything else you can think of. Love starts at home—your home.

Think on This

Disciplining ourselves—learning when to say something and when to keep quiet—is one of the greatest characteristics of real love. Take inventory as to how you show love. Is discipline—when it is necessary—a measure of your

Insight

Real love—the kind that God demonstrated in touching our lives and the kind that Abraham had for his only son—comes with a price tag attached. Sometimes it is the cost of our personal leisure time, the commitment of energy and listening when we would rather be doing something else. Love is expensive but it reaps great rewards ten to twenty years downstream.

love just as much as wiping a child's feverish brow and doing the cooking, cleaning and laundry? How do you express love?

Resource Reading

Genesis 22

Late Starters

"After three days they found him in the temple courts, sitting among the teachers, listening to them and asking them questions. Everyone who heard him was amazed at his understanding and his answers." (Luke 2:46-47)

So you have a youngster who seems to have an attention deficit, do you? It's hard for him to sit still, and he doesn't pay attention to what the teacher is saying. Your child lives in his own private world and doesn't seem to be interested in joining the human club. Before you see your doctor, give serious thought to the accomplishments of the following individuals who were considered slow learners or even retarded before genius began to blossom.

Late starter #1: Thomas Alva Edison, eventually called "The Wizard of Menlo Park." When he was in grade school, his teacher wrote his mother that he should be switched to remedial school because he was "inattentive, indolent" and his brain was "seriously 'addled.'" That incident ended his three months of formal education. The fact that Edison later became quite deaf (perhaps the result of sharp blows to his head administered by a train conductor who was less than happy when Edison started a fire aboard his train) didn't help him to develop an outgoing, pleasant personality, either. But Edison was smart, plenty smart, eventually becoming the most prolific inventor of all times.

Late starter #2: Hans Christian Andersen. Born in 1805, this young Dane wasn't worth "the powder to blow him to Helsinki," as one of his contemporaries put it. He was a dreamer. After mediocre achievements in school, he became a ham actor. Then, at the age of thirty, he wrote *Eventyr*—a story for children—and his career began. Today we memorialize the fairy tales of Hans Christian Andersen.

Late starter #3: Louis Pasteur, a French lad, often described as lazy and undirected. And that he was, preferring wandering the fields and fishing to serious academic study. But in his twenties, he discovered the fascination of science, and eventually the world became indebted to Louis Pasteur, whose discovery—called pasteurization—has saved the lives of thousands of children who otherwise would have died from drinking contaminated milk.

> *Unless you are willing to let a youngster be an original, you will never know what he might blossom into.*

Late starter #4: Otto Von Bismark. If you've never heard of him, obviously you aren't German, because this great man took his place in history as "The Iron Chancellor" and gave his country hope in dark days. As a youth, however, Bismark had little promise of success. He was described as a boy "who seemed destined for oblivion. His student life was spent in fighting, wenching and drinking." He is said to have given up alcohol in his twenties because it could no longer make him drunk. Until age thirty, his life seemed to be wasted. Then his values changed. He went into government, and history tells the rest of the story.

The bottom line is that lots of children are "slow starters." But that doesn't mean they are dull or hyperactive. Many are unchallenged. More than a few are bored, not simply inattentive. Sometimes they are two jumps ahead of their teacher, who complains because the youngster "isn't paying attention."

No two children develop at the same rate. What his big brother—or more likely his big sister—did at the same age shouldn't apply to your youngster. As a parent, you should strive to find out where interests and talents are and feed them. Kids learn from their failures, and unless you are willing to let a youngster be an original who isn't a cookie-cutter duplicate of his cousin or the rest of the kids in his class, you will never know what he might blossom into.

All great leaders were not child prodigies. Most of the great people of our day and history had parents—at least a mother—who believed there was something great down inside and were determined to help discover what it was.

Insight

Every child's maturation rate differs, which means that some children considered slow are merely late starters.

Never underestimate the awesome, often undiscovered potential of a child. A Bach, an Edison, an Oppenheimer, a Babe Ruth may be waiting to be unleashed.

Think on This

1. Every child has certain gifts and abilities. Find out where your child excels and encourage the development of that area without ignoring the fundamentals of education.
2. Avoid the danger of comparing your late-starter with other children.
3. If you feel that your late-starter has a learning disability, get professional help so you can help him stay with his age group.

Resource Reading

1 Samuel 1

Developing the Potential in Your Child

*"Then [Moses'] sister asked Pharaoh's daughter, 'Shall
I go and get one of the Hebrew women to nurse the baby
for you?' 'Yes, go,' she answered. And the girl went and
got the baby's mother. Pharaoh's daughter said to her,
'Take this baby and nurse him for me, and I will pay you.' "
(Exodus 2:7-9)*

Are some individuals born with genius ability? Or are geniuses the products of their environment? Is there something in the childhood of some children—say, early in life—that triggers intense brain development? After Einstein's death, scientists examined his brain to see how it was different from other people's, but their prodding didn't really prove anything.

Before you consign your child to the category of "just average," may I quote Glenn Doman, the director of The Institute for the Achievement of Human Potential? He has demonstrated amazing results working with babies and preschool-age children. (Try teaching your two-year-old to read, as Dr. Doman and his colleagues have done!). He says, "Every child born has, at the moment of birth, a greater potential intelligence than Leonardo da Vinci ever used."[1]

In the context of what we know about the expanding human potential, this means that no one can know what tremendous, unheard-of or even unthought-of potential lies in the future of that little bundle you brought into the world.

Are you interested in bringing out the best in your child? The following guidelines are intended just for you.

1. The gift of yourself is the greatest gift you can ever give your son or daughter.

When I was talking to an educator, I asked, "What is the most important thing a parent can do to bring out the best in a child?" Did this gifted professor talk about the importance of computers or books or expensive tutoring? No. The reply was simply, "The greatest thing that parents can give a child is themselves." She labeled many parents as selfish, too concerned with their own agendas and what consumes their time and interests to have much to give to their children.

> "*The greatest thing that parents can give a child is themselves.*"

Children who excel usually have parents who read to them, who spend time with them, who are involved in school functions, who believe in them, who include them in their lives. The child isn't the hub of their existence and their world doesn't rotate on the axis of their child's schedule, but the child knows that a parent cares, and a parent somehow makes time for that child.

2. Bring out the best in your child by fostering your child's sense of curiosity.

Don't give him a pat answer when you can stir up his curiosity to discover something for himself. A recent Nobel Prize winner recently said that his research in the field of science was the result of his mother's encouragement to find out what makes things tick.

If you don't know the answer yourself, help your youngster connect with those who do. As a boy, my son Steve was fascinated with electronics, a field I knew very little about. But I introduced Steve to Byrd Brunemeier, who was a brilliant electrical engineer. I bought the transistors and components and Byrd helped him learn to put them together. Today Steve is a biomedical engineer!

3. Give your child a faith in God and a moral foundation that can guide his life.

Apart from this we produce gifted children who are morally bankrupt. Bringing out the potential in your child has to include learning how to live, not just how to make a living. It includes the moral, the physical and the spiritual. Integrity, honesty, trustworthiness and faithfulness are all part of what counts in life. Never, never forget it.

> Insight
>
> *While you as a parent cannot do a great deal to increase your child's IQ, you can make a large difference in satisfying his CQ (curiosity quotient), maximizing his potential development.*

Think on This

1. Thomas Edison used to say that his achievements were not the result of his great intelligence but his tenacity and persistence. How do you handle those "Where?" and "How?" questions of your smaller children?
2. Answering a child's question is good. But helping a child discover the answer for himself is much better.
3. What resources do you have in your home to help develop your child's potential? A word of warning: Unscrupulous individuals taking advantage of your desire to give your child the best may strive to sell you "a bill of goods" which is practically worthless when it comes to real education benefit. Before you buy, check with parents who have used those resources.
4. If you don't know how to use the Internet for research, find out. Check out web sites such as www.askjeeves.com.

Resource Reading

John 1:41-51

The Effectiveness of "Program Mom"

*"As a mother comforts her child, so will I
comfort you; and you will be comforted
over Jerusalem." (Isaiah 66:13)*

"In the last decade," writes Delbert Elliott in an article entitled "How Could This Happen?," "we have achieved a major breakthrough in our understanding of the causes of youth violence and the development of effective programs and strategies to prevent violence. Research has succeeded in demonstrating the effectiveness of selected programs in preventing or deterring crime and violence."[2]

The full-page article focused on the wonderful programs now available that are a deterrent to youth violence. While my comments are not meant to detract from these programs, I am glad to tell you that there is an old program which is still unrivaled in its effectiveness. It is called "Program Mom," and frankly, applied in the right places and at the proper times, no program in the entire world can equal its power!

When Program Mom is working, there is a proper tension between love and compassion and motivation and persuasion. I had the most wonderful mother in the world, yet there were times when she could be downright cruel, insisting that I practice my music lessons and that I take a bath (at least on Saturday nights). She insisted that I eat at least a spoonful of everything that was served, actually trying to convince me and my equally disbelieving brother that the spinach was good for us and that turnips and beets (yes, to this day I remain unconvinced) are nutritious. Sure!

More than a few times, she actually sent the two of us in search of a switch, not understanding that to lay this on our backsides would naturally maim us psychologically for life. Thinking of our futures, several times my brother Orville and I would take our pen knives and place a few notches on the switch she trusted us to secure, making certain that it would break with a couple of whacks.

> *hen Program Mom is working, there is a proper tension between love and compassion and motivation and persuasion.*

Seldom did she ever cry, but one time she did. The two of us will never forget it. That was when my dad brought my mother a vase from Marshall Fields in Chicago, and a baseball thrown poorly by one of us went astray and hit the vase, sending that lovely, frilly blue vase to the floor in more pieces than Humpty Dumpty's men or the two of us could ever put together again.

While dad ranted and raved and gave us lectures which we promptly forgot, Mom prayed for us, loved us and showed us that a woman can be involved in business, run the family, listen to us and manage to keep a sense of humor.

She was no pushover, believe me. I have never seen her so angry as the time a man lied to her, telling her that the woman he was with was his wife, when, in fact, he was checking into the motel my parents owned with someone else. Calling him on the phone, she said, "I'll give you five minutes to get out of here, and if you are not gone by then, I am calling your wife to tell her where you are." Believe me, that man and the woman he was with never dressed so fast in their lives.

> ## Insight
>
> *All mothers are human, yet with all their failures, they are one of God's greatest gifts to us. If you are a mother, remember that you are coming through even when you have bad days.*

Good stuff, that program my mom had. Mothers who mother are the greatest program God ever invented. When Program Mom gets into full operation, demons tremble, people get out of the way, and kids learn very quickly that the fury of a tornado is not her equal. Yes, the government programs might help, but give us more Program Moms!

Think on This

1. Don't expect to walk on water. Your mother didn't and neither will you. Each day strive to be the mother who makes a difference in the life of your youngster.

2. When your schedule gets loaded and you find yourself uptight and stressed out, realize you transfer that to your

child and his behavior is a reflection of your attitude. Back off. Take a deep breath and get a new grip on yourself and God.

Resource Reading

Proverbs 31

Accepting Responsibility for Your Children

"For what will it profit a man if he gains the whole world, and loses his own soul?" (Mark 8:36 NKJV)

If a skeptic should ask me for proof that the Bible is a supernatural book, among the reasons that I should proffer is this one, unmistakable fact: this book never glossed over human failure but revealed in accurate detail the mistakes and derelictions of men, telling it exactly as it was.

Each June we set aside one Sunday to honor dads. We call it Father's Day. Naturally dads think this is a great idea. But there is a tragedy to it too, because the failure of fathers today is an enormous social blight.

The emasculation of men began a generation ago when the feminist movement began to tell us that parenting is a non-gender issue, that you are much better off to be single than to be in a marriage which is less than ideal. A great many men, however, can't blame the feminists for their failures. They have only themselves to blame. They haven't been there because they were climbing the corporate ladder, striving to prove their self-worth or to make enough money to bring "the good life."

Their kids don't agree. The son of a prominent executive described his dad as a Phi Beta Kappa, a Rhodes Scholar and a company president who flunked marriage, fatherhood, friendship and fun.

Jesus said, "For what will it profit a man if he gains the whole world, and loses his own soul?" (Mark 8:36, NKJV). He might add, "For what will it profit a man if he gains the company presidency and loses his family in the process?"

Is success—the kind which brings membership in the club, the car and the status—really worth the cost?

> *Home and family come second for the typical corporate executive.*

The *Wall Street Journal,* in conjunction with the Gallup Organization, surveyed the heads of 780 major corporations, focusing on their work habits and attitudes and how men coped with the pressures in relationship to their marriages and their children. The survey was based on interviews with CEOs among the 1,300 largest corporations. It included 100 of the Fortune 500 companies, 276 heads of medium-size companies and 198 independent owners of small businesses.

And how are men coping with success? The survey delivers an unmistakable verdict: home and family come second for the typical corporate executive.

Among the specific findings: chief executives typically work sixty to seventy hours a week, travel six to ten days a month and give up many of their weekends for business meetings. Having made it to the top, two out of every three executives said they were convinced the pressures were greater and the cost to their family more severe than when they were middle managers. One company president quipped, "I gave my family everything in the world but myself."

Your children are pleading, "Dear Dad, please give us yourself, your time and your undivided attention. Please show us the way by being there, by listening when we need to talk, by giving us guidance when we stray, by being God's man so we can understand who we are and who God is."

"Daddy, how much do you make an hour?" asked one little boy. And his father told him. Five minutes later, the boy appeared with his piggy bank and said, "Daddy, here's all my money—just half of what you make in an hour. Now can I have you for just thirty minutes?"

The whole experience of being a dad and father goes by so quickly that you look back and ask, "Where was I when my child was growing up?" There are no second chances, no retakes—only memories. The best of intentions will never suffice for missed opportunities. If God has made you a dad, rise to the challenge. You'll never regret it.

> ## Insight
> A man's greatest achievement is not what he does in business but what he does with his marriage and family.

Think on This

1. If you had made a commitment to your son to be there for opening day of the Little League baseball season and your boss asked you to play golf with an important client at the same time, what would you do? Would you feel torn?
2. A wife complained that her husband was "never there" for his boys as they grew up. His retort was, "No, because you

were never satisfied with what I was able to make so I had to work longer hours to make enough to keep you happy." What is wrong in this situation?

3. Have you as a husband and wife ever sat down and evaluated your priorities? You might start with your checkbook. We spend money on what we consider important.

Resource Reading
Proverbs 3

Dad, Please Love Us

"If anyone does not provide for his own,
and especially for those of his household,
he has denied the faith and is worse than
an unbeliever." (1 Timothy 5:8, NKJV)

A dad may provide leadership for a family without love, but he cannot really love them without providing a measure of leadership. The genuine article is not a wishy-washy emotion associated with weak-kneed men who are more "Milquetoast" than "macho"! The real thing is costly stuff that provides the family with the strength it needs to stand the storm.

"Dad, please love us!" In previous selections, I pointed out that the first mention of the word "love" in the Bible is that of a father in relationship to his son—Abraham's love for his son Isaac.

When Jesus was here in the flesh, He surrounded Himself with twelve men—men who were *men*—and told them to love each other as He Himself had loved them. It was not a sickly, sentimental love and certainly not a sexual love, but a deep commitment to each other which reflected care and concern.

Paul instructed men to "love their wives as their own bodies" (Ephesians 5:28). Long ago Jeremy Taylor wrote, "He that loves not his wife and children feeds a lioness at home and broods a nest of sorrow."

Psychologist Dr. Irene Kassorla, writing for *Family Circle* magazine, says, "I urge parents to kiss and embrace their sons and forget our American nonsense concerning the male macho image! Affection acts as an emotional growth stimulant. Everyone needs it, regardless of age or sex!"

> "*He that loves not his wife and children feeds a lioness at home and broods a nest of sorrow.*"

Love means commitment to someone to meet his needs in such a way that will require personal sacrifice. If you love someone, you care for that person—which is why Paul wrote that husbands should love their wives as their own bodies. A normal male wants to take care of his body, and in the same way he should care for his family. Writing to Timothy, Paul penned some pretty strong words when he wrote this: "If anyone does not provide for his own, and especially for those of his household, he has denied the faith and is worse than an unbeliever" (1 Timothy 5:8, NKJV).

In his book *If I Were Starting My Family Again*, author John Drescher asked himself what he would do if, as the book title suggests, he were starting all over again. He answers that question:

I would love the mother of my children more. That is, I would be more free to let my children see that I love her. To let my child know that I love his mother, I would seek to be faithful in doing little loving things for her. True love is visible. I would show special kindness such as opening the car door, placing a chair at the table, and giving her little gifts on special occasions and writing her love letters when I am gone from home. . . . When a child knows parents love each other there is a security, stability and sacredness about life which is gained in no other way. A child who knows his parents love each other and hears them expressing words of love for each other needs little explanation about God's character of love or the beauty of sex.[3]

One closing thought: it is well and good to talk about love's commitment, care and concern, but love does not come in capsules or in doses. It is born in your heart as God touches your life. Do you want to love your wife and your children more? Then love God more and the latter will follow. "God," wrote Paul, "has poured out his love into our hearts by the Holy Spirit, whom he has given us" (Romans 5:5).

"Yes, Dad, please love us!" Signed, "your family."

Insight

In recent days men have been trying to rediscover who they are and what they are. Through renewal, like what is happening to the thousands of men involved in Promise Keepers, men are discovering that to love is not unmanly or sissy. It is strength, not weakness. Find out how to let out what God put in your heart.

Think on This

1. Do you as a dad hug and kiss your children? If not, why?
2. Are you and your wife (or husband) together in affirming the importance of your love for each other? If not, is this not a problem that needs to be addressed? The

greatest gift you can give your children is to love your spouse.

Resource Reading

2 Timothy 2:1-7

Dad, Please Listen to Us

"He who answers before listening—that is his folly and his shame." (Proverbs 18:13)

"My dad won't listen to me!" says a frustrated teenager. I do not know how many times I have heard those words, at times coming from teenagers whose fathers I know personally. I know that the father really does love his child. He would die for her. So why does he not listen?

Perhaps he does listen, and there is a conflict of signals. The daughter interprets his answer, "No, you cannot do that," as inattention. But perhaps the father *does not really listen*. Perhaps he is too tired at the end of the day; perhaps he does not have the emotional energy to be an effective communicator. Perhaps he just doesn't care about what she is saying.

One of the most important things you can do as a father is to turn off the TV set, put down the newspaper and give your undivided attention to your children. Listen to them without being judgmental or reproving them. You cannot start over, but you can start today. If you want to become the dad God wants you to be, learn to listen to your children. If you do, they will listen to you when they become teenagers and young adults.

I am thinking of one dad who was reading his paper as his little boy, about five years old, was trying to show his father the scratch on his finger. Finally, after repeated attempts to get his father's attention, the dad stopped reading and half yelled, "Well, I cannot do anything about it, can I?"

"Yes, Daddy," the little guy said, "you could have said, 'Oh!' "

> *One of the most important things you can do as a father is to give your undivided attention to your children.*

Do you want to know how to be a better communicator, Dad? Then take note of the following guidelines.

First, realize you *must* recognize the absolute necessity of listening to your family.

It means flopping down on the bed with your teenager and asking, "How did your day go?" It means the willingness to expend time and energy when you would rather be sleeping or reading or whatever. It means that listening is a vital part of being a Christian dad.

Second, learn to listen without intimidating.

There are times when judgmental attitudes or "iron-fisted pronouncements" put an abrupt end to the communicating process. That does not mean that there is not a time and a way in which you can give correction or guidance, but often it is not when you are trying to listen.

Third, show a sincere interest in what your family wants to talk about.

If you live in your own little world, you are apt to find yourself pretty lonely in a few years.

I have come to the conclusion that at every stage of life the immediate challenge is the greatest one in all the world. To a four-year-old, it may be the broken toy he holds in his hand; to a forty-year-old, it may be a company merger. But to the child the problem is as great as is the problem to the dad.

In the final analysis, listening requires a certain posture of the heart, a certain humility of the spirit, a certain interest in someone other than yourself. If this is meaningful to you, then do something about it. Give your children your undivided attention, and listen. It helps fulfill a deep and basic need. Remember, Dad, your family is crying, "Lead us, love us and listen to us." It is a plea that you cannot afford to ignore.

Insight

Listening is a teaching experience. You convey your belief that the person to whom you are listening—whether it is a four-year-old or a business associate—is a person of value and worth. It says, "I care about you enough to give you my complete, undivided attention."

Think on This

1. If you are brave, sit down with your older children and say, "On a scale of 1 to 10, how would you rate me as a listener?"

2. Dad, if your child had a problem, would he: 1. Tell your wife? 2. Tell you? 3. Tell a friend? If he would not tell you, why not?
3. The stage has to be set for the "listening" experience, which means shutting out the interruptions of the household. Pick up on those nonverbal signals that say, "I would like to tell you something. Will you listen?" It's amazing what you may discover.

Resource Reading

2 Timothy 4:10-17

Mistakes Parents Can't Afford to Make

*"The wolf also shall dwell with the lamb, and the
leopard shall lie down with the kid; and the calf
and the young lion and the fatling together; and
a little child shall lead them." (Isaiah 11:6, KJV)*

No parent lives long enough to make all the mistakes in the book, but having been through the process three times over, I've learned there are some mistakes you can't afford to make. The following are statements which should never (no exceptions) come from the lips of a parent.

1. "Do what I say, not what I do!"

Forget it. Your example cancels out everything you say. Your kids need role models, not sermons. If you don't measure up, forget the rhetoric and concentrate on your example.

2. "I want you to have this gift since I can't be there with you."

Gifts are a poor substitute for your presence. Being at the ball game or at the school function, even though it is a sacrifice of time and energy, means more than the reward you may give to your son or daughter.

3. "If you do this again, you're going to get it."

Major blunder! Consistency in parenting is one of the most necessary ingredients. When you do not deal with a situation and discipline a child right away—no matter how tired you are—you are sending conflicting signals. This produces uncertainty. Boundaries which are consistent and definite give stability and security to a child.

> *Teaching a child to be responsible is planting the seeds of future success.*

4. "Because I love you, I'm doing this for you."

Love isn't the issue. Responsibility is. Failing to teach your children to assume responsibility for their lives shortchanges them. Later on, college roommates, bosses or spouses won't do it for them. Teaching a child to be responsible is planting the seeds of future success.

5. "How could you be so dumb?"

Telling a child what he did wrong only certifies the obvious. It's better to talk about how to handle a troublesome situation in the future. Saying, "Let's talk about how you are going to handle this the next time . . ." gives you a chance to deal with character building.

6. "If your older brother can get A's, why can't you?"

Comparing children creates anger and defensiveness. Every child is different. Each has aptitudes and abilities which may be lacking in other children—even children with the same mother and father. Strive to recognize what each child does well and build on that. That's what Scripture is driving at when it says, "Train a child in the way he should go" (Proverbs 22:6).

7. "If you don't stop that, I'll tell your father when he gets home."

Discipline should be administered at the point of wrongdoing by the parent who is aware of the problem, not later when the other parent gets home, or even on the next weekend when Uncle Bill comes for a visit.

8. "If you are a good child, I'll give you some extra money!"

Rewards for doing the right thing teach the wrong thing. Doing right is a responsibility—yes, even a duty. It isn't always rewarded in life by pay increases or bonuses. Teaching children to do right because it is right is responsible parenting.

9. "God's going to get you when you are bad!"

Parents who use God as the "bogey man" are teaching the wrong thing about God. Understanding that there is forgiveness with God as well as with each other is an important spiritual truth.

> *Insight*
>
> Taking a deep breath and pausing for a moment before you say what you want to say may well prevent you from coming up with one of these ten negative statements. Sarcasm and negative comments are always wrong. They produce anger, not correction; resentment, not instruction.

10. "When you get old enough to choose for yourself, you can go to church."

Wrong again! A child learns half of everything he knows by age three, three-fourths by age seven. The spiritual training of a child begins at birth.

Nobody's perfect, but these are some mistakes you can't afford to make.

Think on This

Take inventory. Do you find yourself saying stupid things—things which you really don't mean but say because you are under stress, in a hurry or just plain annoyed? Disciplining yourself is the key to teaching a child how to discipline himself.

Resource Reading
Genesis 20

Out of the Mouths of Babes

"The things that come out of the mouth
come from the heart." (Matthew 15:18)

A husband came home to find his wife in tears. "What's the matter, honey?" he asked.

"Let me tell you," she began. "Today Junior cut his first tooth and took his first step."

"That sounds wonderful," said the baby's father. "Why the tears?"

"Well," continued the wife, "he also had his first fall and cut his lip, and when he did, he said his first bad word."

There is really nothing funny about the implications of a situation a Guidelines listener described when he wrote the following: "I am experiencing a terrible, terrible temper. I can get very violent and I curse and yell very loud. What makes this behavior even worse is that I have a two-year-old who now says curse words, and a month-old baby who will learn them if I can't stop this behavior."

Out of the mouths of babes may come words which shock hearers, words which innocent children neither understand nor mean. We parents, by our examples, are the great teachers of our children. It is both unfair and difficult for a parent to discipline a child for using words he learned from the parent.

In my file is an article by an unknown author which says it so clearly:

If a child lives with criticism, he learns to condemn.
If a child lives with hostility, he learns to fight.
If a child lives with ridicule, he learns to be shy.
If a child lives with shame, he learns to feel guilty.
If a child lives with tolerance, he learns to be patient.
If a child lives with encouragement, he learns confidence.
If a child lives with praise, he learns to appreciate.
If a child lives with fairness, he learns justice.
If a child lives with security, he learns to have faith.
If a child lives with approval, he learns to like himself.
If a child lives with acceptance and friendship, he learns to
   find love in the world.

> *The real failure that confronts our children today is the failure of parents to provide an example for our children to follow.*

We may condemn our schools for failing to provide a wholesome environment for learning. We may condemn the media for the steady diet of antifamily values. But the real failure that confronts our children today is the failure of parents to model the message and provide an example for our children to follow.

Yes, I understand the stress and frustration of a single parent, pressed by inadequate finances, wearied by the constant push of the schedule and the loneliness of going it alone. But the real problem confronting our children today is us. When we parents have our act together, our kids are more secure. When we parents ourselves learn discipline, our children require less discipline. When we learn how to make peace with the circumstances of our lives, our children learn to cope with the frustrations that surround them.

When Jesus talked about the issues of life, He always spoke of the heart. He stressed the fact that what we say and what we do are an extension of what we think in our hearts. In doing verbal combat with His detractors who wanted to observe the legalism of washing their hands when their hearts were impure, Jesus said,

The things that come out of the mouth come from the heart. . . . For out of the heart come evil thoughts, murder, adultery, sexual immorality, theft, false testimony, slander. These are what make a man "unclean"; but eating with unwashed hands does not make him "unclean." (Matthew 15:18-20)

If you, as a parent, are struggling with your own personal life, get help in coping with the pressures that confront you. Remember, it is

Insight

It is unfair to expect our children to adopt a standard which we fail to meet. If you fail in a certain area, begin by asking for God's forgiveness and help, then back off and look at the stress in your life. Learn to pour out your frustration in prayer. Join a support group. Talk.

your heart, not your mouth, which is the heart of the real issue.

Think on This

It is amazing how children read us adults, sensing our anger, our frustration, our compassion and our concern, and then emulate our attitudes and emotions. Should you fail, apologize—right away!—for your failure, thereby teaching an important character-building lesson. Then strive to say and do the right things.

Resource Reading

Matthew 15

Start 'Em Young

"And Jesus grew in wisdom and stature,
and in favor with God and men." (Luke 2:52)

The time to start a child on a musical career is not too far beyond the bootie and bottle age—so says the increasingly popular Suzuki method of teaching music. This approach, originated by Dr. Shinichi Suzuki of Japan, is based on the idea that the earlier the child is exposed to music, the better a musician he will be.

For example, just as a child imitates gestures, he can also imitate music. While Dr. Suzuki likes to start his students in classes between the ages of two and four, he begins exposing them to music even earlier.

If the value of early training is so vital in music, how much more is this true in regard to your child's character! Dr. Suzuki says it is extremely important that a child hear nothing but good music from a very early age. By this he begins to develop a sense of harmony and rhythm.

What do children hear in your home? I am not talking about just music, but everything. Is it good? What do they listen to on TV and radio? What kind of language do they hear and see? Your child will forget a great deal of what you tell him, but he will never forget the example you set in your personal life. At a very early age he knows what is important to you—whether it is your job, your appearance, your home or whatever. You cannot start too early to create an environment at home that teaches the importance of not only good music but high ideals, such as honesty, integrity and respect for authority. What they see at home is "catching."

Going a step further, what does the example set in your home teach about God and the Bible? You may say, "Oh, I take my children to church every Sunday." Do you? That is good! Many parents do not feel it is important enough for them to bother. But what goes on in your home the other six days of the week? More and more, homes are places only to change clothes, eat and sleep.

When God is real to you, He will seem very real to your children.

Problems among children and youth are on the increase. We need all the help we can get in raising our children. Learn to take a few minutes each day to pray together as a family and to read a few verses from the Bible. You may feel awkward or even a little embarrassed or old-fashioned at first, but as you take the first step, God will help you. When God is real to you, He will seem very real to your children. Do not be tricked into thinking that you can wait until they are older to teach them.

The Apostle Paul wrote two letters to a young man named Timothy. This young man was fortunate—he had a godly mother and grandmother who taught him the Word of God. He also sat under Paul's teaching. Of Timothy, Paul said that from a child he knew the Holy Scriptures (see 2 Timothy 3:15). Could this be said of your children?

You go to a great deal of work to raise your children. You teach them good health habits. You spend a great deal of money giving them a good education. Do not shortchange them when it comes to spiritual things. God's Word, the Bible, provides the spiritual guidance your children need in life. It builds integrity and gives them the guidelines to live useful, purposeful lives.

Listen to your three-year-old recite or sing back the commercials he hears on TV. Why not start planting Scripture and songs of the faith in your child's heart? Don't wait. Start 'em young as Dr. Suzuki does with budding musicians. You'll be glad you did!

Insight

In all of life's experiences we never learn more quickly and more diversely than we do in the first three or four years of life—the time to begin planting Scripture, integrity, moral uprightness and a sense of right and wrong.

Think on This

1. If you have a child under five, ask him, "Who was Moses? What beautiful queen of Persia rescued God's people from certain destruction? How many apostles did Jesus have? What does John 3:16 tell us?" Will your child know the answers?

2. What biblical resources do you have to help provide instruction and teaching for your children? If you are too tired to have devotions with your children at bedtime, decide what is the best time for you and dedicate a few min-

utes every day to combating the negative influences of our culture and world.

Resource Reading

Luke 2:41-52

Spying on Your Kids

"Don't keep on scolding and nagging your children,
making them angry and resentful. Rather, bring them
up with the loving discipline the Lord himself approves,
with suggestions and godly advice." (Ephesians 6:4, TLB)

"Is it OK to spy on your kids?" asked the concerned parent of a teenager who isn't talking much, at least not to his parents. How far do you go to find out what is going on in the life of your teenager? Does a teenager have a right not to tell just as he has a right to privacy?

These are some of the issues that are being discussed today by parents who are concerned about drugs and alcohol, about sexual encounters, about being shut out of their teen's world. Those issues include going through your teenager's dresser drawers, reading his diary, going into the storage files of his computer and reading his e-mail (or mail) or otherwise exploring what he thinks you will never see. How far is too far?

Years ago most parents knew what was going on in the lives of their kids, and if they didn't know, it was because they chose not to know. Today, however, it is different. Many of today's teenagers were raised with little contact with their parents. They were dropped off at childcare centers, came home to empty houses and were baby-sat by Nintendo and MTV. It is no wonder that today they give one-word answers to the indifferent questions of parents, rolling their eyes and saying whatever is necessary to get their parents off their backs.

A generation ago when we used the term "spy," images of Agent 007 were conjured up. You spy on the enemy, not your allies. When parents feel it is necessary to spy on their kids, they have drawn a line and put their offspring on the other side as an adversary.

> *When parents have been there for their kids, they can generally read them like a book.*

A teenager doesn't suddenly transform into a silent stranger—he becomes a teenager one day at a time. When parents have been there for their kids, they can generally read them like a book. They know when something is wrong, when there's something that needs to be talked about.

Relationships are what parenting and life are about. You don't have to be concerned about spying when you as a parent nurture the relationship you have with your offspring. You can foster this by doing things together, by participating in hobbies you both enjoy and by knowing what kind of music and books your teen is reading. You can invite your teen's friends over so you get to know them. By having meals together as a family and by going to church together, you can even make it easy for your teen to spend time with friends that are good and tough to be with kids that bring out the worst in him.

I'm including a kind of disclaimer from Dr. Laura Schlessinger on this subject. Says this popular, no-nonsense dispenser of personal advice:

Parents are to respect their children's nest and "stuff." However, when a parent has reason to believe that there might be a problem—sex, drugs, criminality, for example—it is their obligation to use whatever means necessary to help and protect their child.[4]

I agree. Spying is a desperate, last-ditch way of finding out what is happening in the life of a teenager. Much better is heads-up, straight-talk communication, sometimes confrontation and a lot of being there which shows you care.

Insight

Spying does an end run around the relationship of trust you have with your child; however, if your teenager has violated that relationship and the wall of trust has broken down, you have the responsibility to know what he is doing and thinking. But moving into the arena of surveillance brings consequences you need to think through before you start snooping.

And when that kind of parenting is practiced, spying and espionage aren't necessary.

Think on This

1. If you are more comfortable not knowing what is going on in the life of your teenager, you are probably shirking your responsibility to provide guidance and support. If you honestly don't want to know, why?
2. If your teenager began flashing rolls of money and you had no idea where it came from, how would you handle the sit-

uation? If you confronted the issue and got "Don't ask me 'cause I won't tell you" answers, would that be reason to start investigating?

3. Under what circumstances would you feel justified in checking e-mail, phone messages, desk drawers or whatever?

Resource Reading

1 Chronicles 6:1, 6-8

Your Children's Future

*"And I will pour out on the house of David and the
inhabitants of Jerusalem a spirit of grace and supplication.
They will look on me, the one they have pierced, and they
will mourn for him as one mourns for an only child, and
grieve bitterly for him as one grieves for a firstborn son."*
(Zechariah 12:10)

"My name is Igor. If you find me, please bring me to
the following address," began a note Aida
Cerkez wrote and placed in the backpack of her two-year-old
son. Along with the note were two diapers, some crackers,
juice, her life insurance policy and snapshots of Igor and his
mother and father.

Igor lived in Sarajevo, and his mother was so uncertain that
she would be living by the end of the day that she placed the
backpack on the little boy every morning. She said, "I thought
that if we all get killed, he could survive on his own for
twenty-four hours until someone found him, because I taught
him how to open his crackers."

Igor's mother was doing her best to prepare her child to
survive even though she might not make it herself. As I read
about Igor, I couldn't help thinking of my own little grandson
William, who at the time was just about Igor's age. Frankly,
just thinking of William with his little glasses perched on his
nose, his baseball cap on his head and a backpack with crack-

ers and a note inside brought tears to my eyes. Now, several years later, it still does. I have no idea whether Igor and his mother survived. I hope they did.

Yet there are no guarantees in our world. At times it's a pretty tough place to live. Yes, the fighting in Sarajevo has stopped, but the plight of this mother takes place every day somewhere in this world.

Do you think much about the spiritual heritage you are giving your child?

You know, I admired that mother for taking the precautions that she did, no matter how hard it may have been emotionally. An insurance policy, some money and a few crackers provide for immediate needs. Thinking about Igor made me think of what parents do for the future of their children. They provide food, clothing, education, recreation and even culture. They get medical and dental attention for their children. They provide for the physical and emotional needs of their children, but many stop right there.

I'm thinking of a mother of several children whose grandmother picked the children up on Sunday mornings and took them to church with her. The mother slept in on Sundays and did nothing to help the children get ready. "I don't believe in forcing God on my children," she told me. "When they get old enough, they can decide for themselves."

"Do you force them to go to school when they want to play hooky? Do you insist they take baths and medication when they're sick?" I asked.

It is no wonder we are living in a spiritual jungle today. Scores of young men and women are wandering in the dark valleys of life, drifting without meaning and purpose in life. Somewhere in the process of growing up, they were abandoned by parents who gave them little, if any, spiritual direction and haven't found themselves—or God either.

Do you think much about the spiritual heritage you are giving your child? Or should I say "denying your child"? Giving your children a vibrant faith in God is just

Insight

God has given you the opportunity to lay a foundation for your children—much like the root system of a tree which can either go deep into the ground or remain in shallow ground near the surface.

as vital as anything you could include in a knapsack to keep a toddler alive until someone finds him and delivers him to the next of kin.

We assume that our children will learn values just by growing up in a good home. Yet we don't apply that assumption to their education, health, sports or culture. You have eighteen years to pack your child's knapsack before he really faces the world. Make sure you've provided what he needs to survive. It's a jungle out there.

Think on This

You are the value system your child will have in his life. How seriously do you take this truth? Take some time for reflection. It's never too late to do an "in-flight correction."

Resource Reading

Proverbs 20

Public School, Christian School or Home School?

"The sayings of King Lemuel—an oracle his mother taught him." (Proverbs 31:1)

For many parents, there are two options: you either send your youngster to public school and strive to optimize the situation, making the best of what you have, or your youngster will not get an education. *Issue closed.*

But for others, there are some options. You have a choice. Should you opt to pull your youngster out of the liberal, secular system and put him into a Christian school? Many parents do—some at great financial cost—because they are convinced that having their children in a school where God is in and evolution is out, opening the day with prayer, having a teacher who is compassionate and caring, and knowing that their youngster will receive a solid academic foundation are worth the personal sacrifice. So you "make do" with fewer clothes, work longer, spend less and believe that your sacrifice will someday be rewarded.

A third option has taken off in the past decade like a locomotive on the downhill run: home schooling.

For years I was not very excited about either private Christian education or home schooling. First, we were paying for public education with tax dollars, and I said, "Why.

pay for the same thing twice?" Then I felt that we as Christians needed to be salt and light—out there in the world where we can make a difference, maintaining our witness.

But as our culture darkened and sinister, evil forces began to make our schools unsafe, and educational competence declined, I began to see how important private Christian schools can be. Knowing that a child is in a Christian environment where teachers are there because of commitment to Christian ideals is important. Teachers in Christian schools are usually motivated by their desire to make a difference in the lives of their students. It's not the salary that is attractive—teacher salaries in Christian schools are usually substantially less than that in secular school systems.

> *A growing home school movement brings mothers together, provides social outlets for the kids and provides a youngster an education which far exceeds anything public education can offer.*

Why object to home schooling? I was not sure all moms could handle it academically, an issue which is still of some concern. I thought that only a superwoman could be teacher, mother and disciplinarian—all wrapped up in one. Then, I was concerned about a youngster's social development. But a growing home school movement brings mothers together, provides social outlets for the kids and provides a youngster an education which far exceeds anything public education can offer.

It frees a child of the social competition, the "I've-got-to-be-just-like-everybody-else" mentality, and gives him an opportunity to follow Sir Edmund Hillary's wild ride in the ice and snow of the South Pole, retrace the route of the Lewis and Clark expedition or build an incandescent globe, following the same pattern as Thomas Edison did.

Believe me, I'm convinced that it can be very beneficial to the student as well as the mother, provided she has the temperament, the education and the time to handle the additional challenge.

If you have options, explore them fully. Make a list of pros and cons for each one. Lay them before the Lord and say, "Father, this child is a gift from You, and I want to help equip him to know You, love You and serve You all His life. Now, Lord, what's the best thing for us all?"

Having seen the quantum leaps forward that one of our grandsons made this year in home schooling, I'm totally

> ### Insight
>
> *Your child is going to get an education regardless of what happens. It may be one of academic excellence or pitiful weakness; however, no matter how good or poor the school system he may be in, your input as a parent can make a tremendous difference.*

convinced. And besides, William has time for sports and hobbies he would never have had any other way.

Think on This

1. Answering your child's questions—"Why do birds sleep in trees? How does electricity work? Why is the ocean salty?" provides learning experiences. Take the time to help your child find out the answers.

2. When you are exhausted it is OK to say, "Save that question until tomorrow and we'll find out." If your youngster forgets, remind him. He then knows you do care and are interested.

Resource Reading

Acts 13

Sit Still, Kid

"The power of the LORD came upon Elijah and, tucking his cloak into his belt, he ran ahead of Ahab all the way to Jezreel." (1 Kings 18:46)

Ryan, four years old, wiggled and squirmed during story time at preschool so he got sent to the office. His mother got a phone call reporting his lack of attention along with the question, "Have you talked to your doctor about this problem?" In other words, consider medicating the little guy. Whoa! Just a minute! Any four-year-old is going to be active. God says, "Move! Wiggle! Squirm! That's the way I made you!" A less-than-exciting teacher says, "Now, sit still!" There's no question who he is going to listen to.

But there is one thing for sure: millions of kids—now as many as one in twenty grade school youngsters—are being medicated daily. A visit to the doctor who may lack pediatric mental health training results in the diagnosis of: "Sounds like this is ADHD" (Attention Deficit Hyperactivity Disorder) and probably a prescription for Ritalin.

Recently Stanford University researchers demonstrated that there may be a difference in brain chemistry in some children diagnosed with ADHD. Unquestionably some children could not function in society without medical help. For them drugs such as Ritalin are wonderful, but for the vast number of parents who think that feeding a child a pill makes him be a good boy, the route of medication is all together too easy a solution.

Have our children become victims of ourselves, our stress, our frustrations, our busyness, our consumer-oriented lifestyles, our failure to be able to throw a ball with our son in the backyard, or sew or bake or even shop together? We're working. We're too tired. We're too consumed with our own interests. So why not fix the problem with a pill?

The answer to so many of these problems is not through biochemistry, valid as it is. It is through changing our thinking and our lifestyles—the way we live, work and function. But we can't turn back the clock of our culture. Neither are there easy solutions to the problems that confront parents today.

> *L*ook at the whole picture before you head to the pharmacy and expect the medication to fix that problem.

Pediatrician Dr. Kathi J. Kemper, who practices holistic medicine, tries to put the whole situation in perspective. She says,

In the old days, kids followed and learned from their parents around the home, farm or other business. There was a fair amount of movement, physical activity and parental involvement, without the modern cultural phenomenon of instant gratification. Nowadays, kids are bombarded with fast food, frenetic television and video games. Modern schools increasingly demand that young children sit quietly in crowded classrooms with few breaks for vigorous physical activity. And busy families just don't have as much time to give children one-on-one attention.[5]

You as a parent must ultimately remember that you are Dr. Mom and Dr. Dad, and that you know your child far better than an overworked physician who takes as much time as his schedule will allow to evaluate but doesn't have the whole picture. Take time. Talk. Get more opinions. Explore alternatives to your working outside the home. Realistically evaluate how much time your child is outdoors as opposed to being in front of a TV or a computer game. Look at the whole picture before you head to the pharmacy and expect the medication to fix that problem.

No, Ryan's mother didn't talk to the doctor. She's my daughter. We blame his wiggling on his DNA. It seems his mother and his grandfather (that's me) used to wiggle and squirm when things got boring as well. Remember, when God says, "Wiggle," and you say, "Sit still," you've got tough competition.

> ## Insight
>
> *When medication is really needed, it is wonderful—a gift from God. But to medicate a child's inattention when he is bored, keyed-up because of inactivity, or fidgety when he is tired is wrong. The problem may well be your lifestyle as a parent.*

Think on This

1. There is safety in the multitude of counselors. Ask your mother how you were as a child.

2. Remember that every child's temperament and personality are different. There are some children who sit remarkably still, but if God made your child with a tighter spring, that doesn't make him defective—just different.

Resource Reading
1 Samuel 2

The Diagnosis May Be Wrong

*"Who is this that darkens
my counsel with words without
knowledge?" (Job 38:2)*

*H*is name is Michael Campareri. He's nine years old. He also happens to be the U.S. National Chess Champion. At the tender age of three, his parents discovered he liked to play chess and seemed pretty good at it too. They bought him a computer chess game. He mastered it. At the age of six, they got a chess coach for him, but he soon quit. His ego was affected when Michael consistently beat him. Today, people of all ages who think they are pretty good at the game get trounced on a regular basis by this young champ.

Recently he took on some twenty young chess players, moving from board to board, quickly knocking them out of the game. "He kills you on the opening move, then he kills you again," said one of them. They described him as a professional, focused and exacting.[6]

And by the way, there is one more thing which you need to know. Michael has been diagnosed with ADD (Attention Deficit Disorder)!

Dr. Kathi J. Kemper, a holistic pediatrician, says that if your child has been diagnosed with ADD (Attention Deficit Disorder) there are several things you need to know. There are changes you can make in your lifestyle and eating habits that can make a big difference. She would also be quick to tell you that every child who has been diagnosed (perhaps like Michael) doesn't really have a problem that needs to be medicated.

Doctors who practice general medicine are trained to see a problem and eliminate it. But doctors who practice holistic medicine attempt to treat the whole person. Dr. Kemper also feels strongly that kids need to know they are not bad simply because they have trouble paying attention. She would quickly tell you that perhaps it is you as a parent who needs help—not your child.[7]

Every child who has been diagnosed with ADD doesn't really have a problem that needs to be medicated.

In evaluating what is happening to our small fry today, I go back to Scripture and ask myself, *Was Elijah also ADD? Was it possible that John the Baptist—antisocial, living in isolation with a diet of locusts and wild honey—could have been diagnosed as having a bipolar disorder? Was Judas suffering from acute depression? Is there nothing in Scripture to which we can relate our problems today?*

There is and there is not. I'm convinced that our lifestyle today has produced all kinds of situations which were never God's intention. Elijah, the twelve who walked with Jesus, those we read about in the New Testament never watched television or played a computer game. For the most part they were outdoors. They lived outdoors, they walked, they exercised and they breathed fresh air.

Of course there is no going back. But this has never changed: God cares. He cares infinitely about you, your child and your well-being. He's there to give you direction and help when you need it.

he title of this selection says it all: the diagnosis may be wrong!

Think on It

1. If your child really does need Ritalin or something else, don't feel guilt.
2. Try to help your youngster know that he is not naughty or bad when it is impossible for him to sit still.

Resource Reading

Job 42

The Balancing Act of Parenting

*"I tell you the truth, anyone who will not receive
the kingdom of God like a little child will
never enter it." (Mark 10:15)*

The young mother yelled at her child, "Be quiet!" A look at the child, under a year of age, told me that the baby was sick. Yes, the mother's nerves were on edge. Her older children had colds too. But the little child couldn't turn off the tears any more than I could sing in Swedish or grow hair on the top of my head now that it has disappeared. What the child did understand, though, was the tone of voice, and the message was negative, very negative.

I didn't say anything, but I began to reflect on the fact that parenting is a constant struggle to maintain balance.

Observation #1: A wise parent has to balance expectations with abilities.

Obviously, the ability of the sick child to stop crying was totally out of balance with the mother's expectations. It was impossible, period. Punishing a child for what he is incapable of doing is not only wrong but also counterproductive to mature development.

"But your older sister can do this math! Why can't you?" The problem is that every child is different, and the fact that an older child may be able to do something doesn't necessarily mean that another child can do the same task at the same age.

Observation #2: The wise parent has to balance love and discipline.

You can discipline a child without love but you can't really love a child without the discipline that says, "I love you too much to let you get away with this (talking back to me, throwing your food all over the table, sticking your tongue out at the teacher)." Does the Bible make a case for discipline? Yes, a strong one. Does it make as strong a case for loving your child? Absolutely. Both are important and both must be balanced.

> *N*ot only is parenting a matter of balance, but so is life itself.

Observation #3: The wise parent has to balance protecting a child from hard knocks and letting him experience the consequences of his actions.

This especially applies to older children. Do you do your youngster's homework for him or let him face school detention for not doing it? Do you lie for your teenager to protect him or let him face the court when he's been drinking? I'm convinced that one of the greatest disservices a parent can do is to fail to help a child understand that with every choice there are consequences, sometimes tough ones.

Observation #4: Successful parenting has to balance turning loose with holding on.

Two mistakes of parenting are being overly strict and overly permissive. Turn a child loose too soon, giving him too much independence, and he will get into trouble, but hold on to the youngster for too long and he's certain to become angry and rebellious.

Not only is parenting a matter of balance, but so is life itself. There is one thing for sure: you as a parent teach your child by what you do, not what you say. When you are out of control, your kids will be out of control. When you yell at your child, he will yell as well. Whatever you do, he's going to do too, but he's going one step beyond where you are or what you do. It's been that way since the days of Adam and Eve, and it's not going to change.

Insight

Parenting is an ongoing process of balancing expectations with reality, bringing out the very best in our children without condemning them for what they cannot do or making them feel inadequate when they cannot rise to our hopes and dreams.

Think on This

When you face a tough decision about your children, talk over the situation with an older, more mature friend—a parent, an older person in your church, a neighbor you respect.

Sometimes hearing someone else tell you what you already know in your heart is affirming and encouraging.

Resource Reading
Proverbs 22

⟳hen Children Become Our Victims

"An angry man stirs up dissension, and a hot-tempered one commits many sins." (Proverbs 29:22)

"⟳s there more child abuse today, or is it simply that we are hearing more about it?" That was the issue I put to a psychologist who also happens to be an ordained minister. Dr. Millard Sall believes that there is more child abuse today than a generation ago, *and* we are hearing more about it.

For a long while some teachers, school administrators and even police felt that what takes place between a parent and a child is personal, and they hated to get involved in domestic affairs. They knew there were some parents who were out of control and took out their anger on their children, but child abuse was a subject that had a social stigma attached to it, and for a long while our indifference scarred the future of thousands of victims.

How much child abuse is there? Only God knows for sure. Estimates range from 2-5 million cases a year, and some feel that the actual number of children who are physically abused in the course of a year is closer to 10 million, depending on how abuse is defined. Many of these incidents, however, still go unreported and unnoticed. Unnoticed, that is, save by the victims who will bear emotional and/or physical scars for the rest of their lives.

Another question I put to Dr. Sall is this: "Just what is child abuse?" Sall believes that physical child abuse is much different than discipline. A willfully disobedient or defiant child can be physically disciplined without bringing blood, causing welts or injuring a child's spirit. The purpose of discipline is to enforce proper behavior, but punishment becomes abusive and can greatly harm a child.

Children become victims of abuse every year. Their physical injuries include burns by cigarette butts, tiny hands placed on a stove, knife wounds, dislocations of limbs and fractures and sexual abuse, which is a whole subject in itself. The emotional injury and trauma can scar a person for life.

We've got to learn how to manage anger and frustration without taking our emotions out on our children.

I, for one, will never forget the shock I encountered when I visited the Los Angeles County Morgue and saw firsthand the horrible results of child abuse. It isn't even fit to write about but it is taking place in our out-of-control society today.

Why are so many innocent children victims today? Health-care workers who are involved with children generally point out that there are three basic reasons:

1. Some parents with personality flaws such as low self-esteem, volatile tempers or a marked lack of patience and self-control will take out their frustrations on those closest in proximity—often their own helpless children.

2. Certain children tend to bring out the worst in their parents. For example, children who are hyperactive by their very natures tend to run full-bore from their waking moment until they drop exhausted. Stress continues to mount as a parent despairs of speaking calmly or rationally.

3. Marital stress, which spans a broad gamut of problems from financial pressures to broken homes, also creates distress and some of that is transferred to children.

> ## Insight
>
> T here is a limit to what you can handle. When you feel that you are being pushed to the boiling or breaking point, you need to get help lest your children become victims.

In simple terms, often parents can't cope, and as a result their children become victims. A sad legacy of child abuse is that victims of child abuse face a far greater chance of growing up and duplicating this vengeful act of aggression on their own children. "All right," you may be thinking to yourself, "the problem exists. What can be done about it?"

First, we need to recognize it is everybody's problem. Ignoring the issue only aggravates the situation. When a child has bruises or welts, black eyes or injuries, someone needs to be held accountable, and our failure to do so not only is a grave injustice to the child but also abets the terrible act of child violence.

Second, we adults facing stress and pressure must learn how to cope. This may require professional help. It requires emotional ventilation through exercise—hard, vigorous exercise; prayer and therapy; and facing the issue clearly. Almost every person knows where his boiling point is, and if you feel that you are capable of losing it, you have to learn to shut off the system or get help before you get out of control.

We can't blame our society, however wrong it is. We must accept responsibility for ourselves today.

Think on This

1. First, don't discipline your child when you are angry even though wrongdoing has taken place. It's unfair to your child and also dangerous.
2. If you were a victim of violence when you were growing up, you have a greater propensity to be violent than the person who had not experienced this as a child.
3. If you—even once—have inappropriately struck, hit or kicked your child, you need professional help. Realizing this and admitting it is the first step.

Resource Reading
Proverbs 29

Christian Values 101

*"Fathers, do not exasperate your children;
instead, bring them up in the training and
instruction of the Lord." (Ephesians 6:4)*

One dad thought that he knew the formula for conveying values to children. He told the press that he really believed a child would turn out just fine if the parents loved the child, spent plenty of time with him, involved him in wholesome activities and helped him get a balanced education. He said, "Suddenly after seventeen years of dedicated effort, something happened to my foolproof plan. I found I was the father of a murderer."

What happened? The son was sentenced to twenty-five years in prison after pleading guilty to the murder of a sixteen-year-old girlfriend who had spurned his advances. The father said, "The shock, agony and soul-searching are unbelievable. Everything you believe in is gone in one bolt of lightning that rips your heart out at the same time. What went wrong? Nothing fits your notions of criminal behavior and what to do about it."

No parent dares be so smug or sure of himself that he can take lightly what this brokenhearted dad told the press. But the question remains, "What went wrong? What caused the son to turn his back on everything his parents believed in?"

Of one thing you can be certain. Every parent, no matter what he does, is conveying a value system to his child—the parent who purposely sets out to convey a positive value system as well as the parent who lets his children take the path of least resistance and do whatever he pleases.

The greatest contributors to a child's value system are his mother and father, at least in the long term. In the short term, it could be his peer group. A child's value system becomes a reflection of the aggregate influences in his life, whether they are what he sees on television and the media, what friends think or the impact that church and God have made in his life. A parent who models the message and reflects the kind of value system in his personal life that he wants his child to embrace is far more effective than a parent who talks about one thing but practices another.

> *Taking time for hobbies, for recreation, for worship, for time together is all part of showing what you think is important.*

The parent who acknowledges personal failure when it happens is also teaching an important lesson: as we confess our sin and failure, our Heavenly Father also forgives us and gives us the strength to overcome. But the parent who pretends to be perfect when in reality he is very fallible is teaching hypocrisy, and our kids pick up on that very quickly.

No parent, however, can convey much of a value system when he is not there. Taking time for hobbies, for recreation, for worship, for time together is all part of showing what you think is important. Don't for a moment confuse quality time with quantity time. They aren't the same, and no stretch of the imagination can convince you that a couple hours on the weekend compensate for your absence Monday through Friday.

Out of the tragedy of the shooting at Columbine High School in Littleton, Colorado in 1999 came the realization that the two young men who so callously took the lives of their classmates were living in a world totally divorced from the one their parents thought they were in. Their parents simply were not aware of what they were thinking, of what was influencing them and how they felt about issues of major importance. Their assumptions were 180 degrees opposed to reality.

When it is all said and done, every child has a will of his own. Regardless, most parents feel personal failure when a child goes wrong. Follow the biblical mandate of raising your child in the discipline and the instruction of the Lord, and then let God do His work in your child's heart. You can trust Him to do His part when you have done yours. He can work in a heart where no one else can!

Insight

To have an accurate "read" on where your teenager is mentally, emotionally and spiritually, you've got to be there with him—not know only that he's in the house, door closed, earphones blaring music (the words of which you have never heard). Time spent one-on-one is the only way to get a feel for what's happening.

Think on This

1. Plan one-on-one time with your youngster. How about a lunch or breakfast date with your daughter? A backpacking or fishing trip with your son? A hobby or work project?
2. Take your DayTimer and note exactly how much time you spent with your son or daughter in the last three months. Now compare that with the time spent with your friends.

Resource Reading

2 Peter 1:3-22

Teaching Honesty to Your Children

*"But mark this: There will be terrible times in the last days.
People will be lovers of themselves, lovers of money,
boastful, proud, abusive, disobedient to their parents,
ungrateful, unholy, without love, unforgiving, slanderous,
without self-control, brutal, not lovers of the good,
treacherous, rash, conceited, lovers of pleasure rather than
lovers of God—having a form of godliness but denying its
power. Have nothing to do with them." (2 Timothy 3:1-5)*

*C*hildren lie for the same reasons that adults lie: to avoid punishment, to win respect, to appear better than they are because they don't trust someone with the truth, or because they feel threatened with power. Without realizing it, many parents teach their children to lie and actually encourage them in the practice.

Want to teach the importance of honesty to your child?

Model honesty yourself.

Children who lie often have parents who lie, and very quickly youngsters learn from their example. They overhear Mom saying on the phone, "No, John isn't at home" when Dad is parked in front of the TV and doesn't want to be disturbed. They pick up on phony excuses you make; they hear you lying to the traffic officer who pulled you over; they understand what the conference is about at the kitchen table as you sweat over your tax forms.

To teach honesty to your child, be honest with him yourself.

When your kids are confronted with a problem, don't expect them to respond with honesty if you aren't honest with them. For example, say you are losing your job and you can't take the family on vacation. But you sugarcoat the whole situation, thinking that you are sparing your child the anguish of knowing you are without work. A child picks up on your stress and your insecurity, and the uncertainty of not knowing what is wrong does far more damage than telling the truth and being explicit.

Here is another example: Your child's grandmother has been felled by a stroke and is hospitalized. Telling your child that everything is all right when he has seen the pain in the family will cause confusion and alarm. Better to establish open communication and take difficulty as an opportunity to point out that we can trust God in difficult situations.

ithout realizing it, many parents teach their children to lie and actually encourage them in the practice.

Don't give your youngster an opportunity to lie; rather, make it easy for him to tell the truth.

Suppose you have laid down certain geographic boundaries and you expect your children to stay within them. But you know for a fact that your child didn't stay within them. Don't say, "Did you go beyond the corner at the end of the block?"

Instead, say, "Why did you go into the next block?" It gives your child a reason to explain his behavior rather than to deny what he did.

However, when parents are overly restrictive, they set the stage for dishonesty. Far better is open and free communication so your child has the freedom to say, "I don't think that you are being fair in what you are doing!" That can be done without malice or anger. Open communication evaluates the situation and allows a youngster to express himself without talking back in a disrespectful manner.

To teach honesty, stress the fact that what others may do is different from what you observe in your family.

Very early in life children begin to understand what truth is. Child psychologists say that by age four most children can sift fantasy from truth. When they have playmates who make it a practice to lie, you must teach your children that honesty is a fundamental matter of trust and love in your family, and help them to understand that when trust is lost, it affects your relationship. If the behavior of other kids begins to rub off, put those kids off limits. Learning that you still love and accept a child

Insight

Children can learn to be dishonest out of fear for the consequences of their actions or by following the example of others. Make sure you model the message of absolute honesty that you want your child to embrace.

when he has behaved unacceptably helps your child to be honest with you, regardless of the consequences.

Honesty is the best policy—it's the only way to build relationships that endure.

Think on This

Before you blame others for influencing your child negatively, ask yourself, "Do I ever have people say, 'No, he's not here' on the telephone when I don't want to talk? Do I bend the truth myself?" Be honest. Here's where you need to begin applying the straight ruler of truth.

Resource Reading

Acts 5:1-10

Your Example

"Therefore everyone who hears these words of mine and puts them into practice is like a wise man who built his house on the rock." (Matthew 7:24)

Some theologians were discussing the merits of different modern Bible translations. Each one seemed to have a favorite and knew several good reasons why his choice was superior to other versions. "King James is archaic," one contended. Another believed that the New International Version takes too much liberty with the text in trying to be relevant.

Overhearing the conversation, another man spoke up and said, "Frankly, I liked my father's translation."

"Oh, did your father translate the New Testament?" asked one of the men, who knew that his father was quite a scholar.

"Yes," he replied. "He translated it into his life, and that's why I'm serving the Lord today!"

The best translation of the Bible is that which is lived out by our examples day by day as we face the realities of living in a broken, sinful world. In recent days we have lamented the moral collapse of our world, often blaming "the system." We denounce secularism, the New Age movement, the moral breakdown of society. Of course, all of this does impact our world and the education system where many of our children spend a considerable part of each weekday.

Yet these forces, sinister and diabolical as they may be, are not destroying our children as much as our failure to teach right from wrong and to convey old-fashioned, God-given values to our children. I'm thinking of a college girl who wrote and said, "My mother objects to my living with my boyfriend, yet she spends weekends with her new boyfriend. What's the difference?"

Values are formed by the environment in which children grow up, including the attitudes as well as the actions of parents. When you live like a devil, you can't expect your children to walk like saints. Recently I heard a child of about three years of age using profanity which I am certain the child couldn't comprehend at all. His language was a reflection of what he heard at home.

Values are formed by the environment in which children grow up, including the attitudes as well as the actions of parents.

No parent chooses the era in which he raises children. To be a parent includes the parameters of the world in which we live. Have you ever considered that those who lived in the early Church, including the disciples who walked with Jesus, didn't have a very easy time raising their children?

But what you can do is choose how you respond to the needs of your child, which forms the framework of a value system. When you hug or show affection to a child, the child knows he is loved. When you take time to read or play with a child, your child grows intellectually. When you pray and read Bible stories to your child, you teach right from wrong. When you live out a code of morality and honesty, your children learn commitment and the importance of love in marriage.

When you show respect to aged parents and law enforcement officials, your children show respect to you. When you attend church and take your children, you show them what is important to you. When you discuss issues and pray together as a family, you are showing that disagreements can be solved without hostility and violence.

There is a place for dissent. There is a time for anger. There are causes that must be defended. There are wrongs that cannot be ignored and must be fought, but all these are no substitute for the presence of a parent who assumes the God-given responsibility of being a parent.

Our children are God's way of saying, "There is hope for the future!" They are our great responsibility.

Insight

Your kids don't expect perfection from you but they do want authenticity. Hearing you say, "I'm sorry for what I did. I was a lousy example for you" teaches an important lesson—Christians are not perfect, just forgiven. As God forgives us, so we must ask for and extend forgiveness to others.

Think on This

1. When you are wrong, admit it. Bluffing your way through a situation when everyone knows you are wrong produces anger and irritation in our children.
2. Strive to be the message you want your kids to see and hear.

Resource Reading

2 Corinthians 3:1-5

Your Influence vs. the Influence of Culture

*"For I have chosen him, so that he will direct his children
and his household after him to keep the way of the LORD
by doing what is right and just, so that the LORD will
bring about for Abraham what he has promised him."*
(Genesis 18:19)

When Judith Rich Harris' book *The Nurture Assumption* was published in 1999, thousands of professionals said she didn't know what she was talking about. Harris contended that it is other kids—not parents—who are influencing teenagers today.[8]

I am convinced that many parents today think they are the major influence in the lives of their kids, when in reality, they provide only a roof over their heads, food on the table and enough spending money to allow the youngster to indulge in about anything he wants—junk food, junk music, junk entertainment and junk friends. Then when a disaster occurs, they cry out, "God, how could this have happened? I've given my child everything money could buy."

What they are missing is the core content of parental involvement—a spiritual connection and communication which is more than, "So you need more money, huh? What did you do with what I just gave you?"

Lynda Madison is a clinical psychologist who works with teens, many of whom have been suicidal. She is convinced that parents think they are communicating with teens when in reality both parents and children tell each other what they think the other wants to hear. A mother says, "How did your day go?" The teenager daughter rolls her eyes—which her mother doesn't see—and replies, "Oh, just fine" as she retreats to her room to call a friend.

Many parents today think they are the major influence in the lives of their kids, when in reality, they provide only material things.

She also believes that teens and their parents would like to know what's going on in each other's lives, but not enough to clear the time, make a commitment and get involved. Polite, meaningless exchanges of trivia become the substitutes of really knowing, deeply caring and being there for the trip.

Family First, an independent, nonprofit research and communications organization, has done extensive research among both parents and teens, exploring the relationship between parents or the absence of them and teenage violence today. Their most recent report says,

> When asked to identify the leading cause of youth violence
> . . . adults and teens disagree. One-third of adults (34%)
> cite *"divorce and fathers who are not involved in their kids' lives,"*
> as the leading cause of youth violence, followed by *"violence*

on TV, in movies, in music and on the Internet" (21%) and *"teen drug use"* (20%).

Teens have slightly different views about the cause of youth violence. One-third (31%) of teens say *"teen drug use"* is the primary cause of youth violence followed by *"access to weapons"* (26%) and *"violence on TV, in movies, in music and on the Internet"* (21%). Significantly fewer teens than adults (11% versus 34% respectively) point to *"divorce and fathers who are not involved in kids' lives"* as the leading cause of youth violence.[9]

Yes, I understand that you can lead a horse to water but you can't make him drink. Yes, I concur that there are times when a parent is there for his kid in school, in church, in activities and at home as well, and the youth turns his back to God and chooses to go the wrong way.

But I also know that for generations, parents have proved what the wise man wrote long ago, that when parents teach and train a child in the way he should go, setting the example in their personal lives, that youngster treads in their footsteps. Occasionally it just takes a while.

Insight

Statistics are not iron-clad, self-fulfilling prophecies as to how your child will go. Godly parents have always held values which contradict the cultures of their day.

Think on This

1. Since a child follows in the footsteps of a parent, it's wise to take a compass and ask yourself where you are headed.
2. It is possible that your youngster is living in an entirely different world than you think. He may say, "Yes, Dad!" or "Sure, Mom," telling you what he thinks you want to hear but doesn't really mean it. How much do you care?

Resource Reading

Matthew 18:1-5

Where Did My Kid Learn This?

*"Be very careful, then, how you live—not as unwise
but as wise, making the most of every opportunity,
because the days are evil." (Ephesians 5:15-16)*

"Dear Dr. Sala," writes a friend of my organization, Guidelines, "I found an [audio] tape where my eleven-year-old son used vulgar language including the 'F' word. Also, I was called by the principal of my thirteen-year-old son's school and was told that he stuck up his middle finger at his teacher. We are supposed to be Christians, and I wonder where my children learned all these things." More than one parent has asked, "What's gone wrong? Where have I failed?"

There is no questioning the fact that parenting is not an easy task. It's tough to get the job done, yet quite often parental failure is as predictable as the sun rising in the east. But the sad thing is that so many parents assume they are communicating values when in reality they are allowing the values of our environment to shape the lives of their children. Then we throw up our hands in dismay and say, "I can't understand what's happened!"

Let's take a look at several of the most powerful forces in the lives of our children and see what kind of input they make.

What's the greatest force in the lives of children today? I don't think anyone would challenge me if I said "the media." John Condry of Cornell University contends that the average child now spends one-third of his waking hours watching television or playing video games on a TV.

In answering the question, "Where are my children learning values?" better take a hard look at the number of hours they sit in front of a television set or a computer screen with unsupervised access to the Internet.

It's easy to blame the media, our children's friends and the educational system for our children's poor behavior when the real cause is our own parental failure.

The second most influential factor in the life of a child is his peer group, which includes the influence of schoolmates. Here the possible influence of a parent is lost by default. In nearly fifty percent of our homes, children are spending some period in their lives living with only one parent. Often, long hours, inadequate quality time and the lack of an authority figure leaves a child on his own much of the time. The major influences become youthful friends. An empty house, unsupervised activities and boredom combine to bring out the worst in a child striving to find approval and support by his peer group.

The third influence is school. School was once a place where a child could receive positive moral and social input, but today many teachers strive just to make it through the day without too much hassle. Sometimes a teacher will even use profanity—but let a teacher talk about God or the Ten Commandments, and he's subject to reproof and censure. Kids become streetwise but lack real educational fundamentals. Leaving God out of the classroom doesn't leave morality out, but the kind of moral issues which are often discussed contradict family values such as monogamous commitment and heterosexual relationships.

What about the influence of a parent's life? It's easy to blame the media, our children's friends and the educational system for our children's poor behavior when the real cause is parental failure, our own failure. I understand that not working may not be an option and feeling guilt because you have to be gone only compounds the problem. It's much better to be alert; use the phone to check in and ask questions about who is in the house, what homework has to be done, what's going on.

Before you ask, "How did this happen?" when your kids get in trouble, better take inventory and fight back. It's your responsibility as a parent.

> ### Insight
>
> *Our kids are much more "streetwise" than we were at their age, and subsequently more sophisticated. Helping them think for themselves—as opposed to going with the flow of their peer group—is a positive step forward.*

Think on This

When moral situations confront your family, rather than simply condemning the person who failed, talk about how the situation could have been better handled. Ask, "Is there any-thing we could have done differently?"

Resource Reading

1 Corinthians 6:9-20

Conveying Values to Your Children

*"Know therefore that the LORD your God is God;
he is the faithful God, keeping his covenant of love
to a thousand generations of those who love him
and keep his commands." (Deuteronomy 7:9)*

Interested in conveying a positive value system to your child? First, you and your mate need to be on the same wavelength. Talk about what values are important.

Next, take a look at your environment. What surrounds your child? What are the influences in his life—television, friends, magazines? (By the way, your kid knows everything that goes on in your life. He reads you better than you read him. He knows what's in the bottom drawer of your cabinet as well as the top shelf in your closet.)

Then—evaluate the people who influence your child. Who are they? Next to you as a parent, who would you say has the greatest influence in your child's life? A babysitter? The boy down the street? The neighbor children who watch TV with your child before you come home from work?

Would you include grandparents? It is amazing what a great influence your extended family can have in the lives of your children. *But they have to be there.* They have to be willing to take the time to invest, not simply reinvest as a second-generation experience. I'm not suggesting they do the "heavy work" of parenting, but reinforce, encourage and be a friend.

The next step is to evaluate what positive biblical teaching and Christian values you are conveying. Television has never had a greater negative impact, but to balance that out, never before has there been so much good, positive stuff available. I'm thinking of the Christian videos and tapes which kids quickly memorize.

Negatively or positively, the most profound impact in any child's life is that of the example of a mother and a dad.

By the way, are you in church on a regular basis? Do you go beyond that, sharing the Bible with your family through family devotions and bedtime stories? If not, why not? No church—no matter how great—can substitute for what you can do at home.

What about your influence in your child's life? Negatively or positively, the most profound impact in any child's life is that of the example of a mother and a dad. Some, in fact, believe that the father's influence, which may not even be as intimate and personal, is even greater than a mother's when it comes to shaping a child's outlook in life. "Daddy," a little boy of about six asked as his mother prepared to take him to Sunday school, "how old do I have to be before I can stay home with you and read the comics?" Enough said.

Being a parent is an awesome responsibility. But it is one of the greatest experiences of life, and it can be one of the most rewarding. You can make it that way. It can still be done.

Think on This

Following the insight to the right, ponder what this means in your family.

Insight

Lacking the maturity that you have as an adult, your child can't handle some things that you can. That's why you need to put some things aside or give them up—a minor sacrifice for your child.

Resource Reading

1 Kings 13

Your Children Are Worth Fighting For!

"Don't be misled; remember that you can't ignore God and get away with it: a man will always reap just the kind of crop he sows!" (Galatians 6:7, TLB)

"What kind of kids are we going to have in another generation?" That question came from a concerned parent and educator as he reflected on the number of children today who are growing up in one-parent homes, whose role models are movie stars and heroes who are more prone to settle scores with violence than negotiation.

Do you ever think much about what the world will be like in another generation, especially if trends which began in the '60s and the '70s continue? If the foundation is destroyed, what hope is there for the house itself?

An old marine story is told about a young man who was carrying the radio when his unit was pinned down by hostile fire. Quickly, he contacted headquarters and was asked what the situation was. He replied, "The enemy is to the north and south; the east and west. Actually," he replied excitedly, "we're surrounded by 'em."

"Well," said the sergeant at headquarters, "What do you think?"

The young man swallowed hard as he replied, "Well, sir, the enemy won't get away from us now!"

That's the way it will be raising children in a hostile world. What can we do to fight back, to help insure that our kids can make it no matter what the shape of the world of the twenty-first century? There's plenty you can do. Fight back with these powerful guidelines:

Teach your child to be his own person.

Help him understand that it's OK to be different, to say no, to resist pressure to conform. If you can win in this, you have passed on to your child a tremendous tool in fighting back in the days and years ahead. Today, peer pressure, going along with the crowd, being like everyone else is one of the most powerful forces confronting children and teenagers. How do you teach a child that it's OK not to go along? You've got to be secure yourself and at peace with your life. Family loyalty and commitment to each other are part of that answer.

> *Help your children understand that it's OK to be different, to say no, to resist pressure to conform.*

Fight back by teaching your child how to manage anger.

"Be ye angry and sin not" (Ephesians 4:26, KJV) is the biblical injunction. This requires both the example of a parent and the patience of a teacher. Note that I didn't say to make your child understand that all anger is wrong. Managing anger means we learn to direct our anger toward situations which are wrong, not at people who challenge us. Angry adults transfer their emotions to children, who in turn take out their hostilities on each other. Nobody gets his way all of the time, and the person who lets a child get away with whatever he wants is not helping that child come to grips with the real world.

Teach your child that there are consequences to every choice and action.

Our choices determine the consequences. It's the cause-and-effect relationship of life. If you choose to cheat, the consequences may be flunking the test. When a child chooses disobedience and he knows that the consequence will be discipline, that child also learns that life rewards or punishes us the same way. The undesirable consequences come with the choice.

This is the way life itself is, and in a real sense, the parent who fails to teach his child that every choice produces consequences short-changes him. Then when he gets out in the real world and discovers that he doesn't study and he flunks, or he fails to attend school and gets expelled, he thinks that the world is unfair. The eternal law of the harvest is that "a man reaps what he sows" (Galatians 6:7).

> ## Insight
>
> *Each of you as a parent is the answer to that question, "What kind of kids are we going to have in another generation?" Your lifestyle becomes the message.*

Fight back by teaching your child that problems can be solved.

There is a solution to every problem. Life is full of challenges and difficulties which can be met.

Fight back by giving your child a value system that distinguishes right from wrong—and chooses the right.

You'll be glad you did. Your kids are worth fighting for!

Think on This

1. If a parent lies for his child, thus saving him from discipline at school, what message does this convey to the child? To the world regarding your character?
2. Keeping communication live and vibrant is important. How do you do this? Can you separate censure from openness?

Resource Reading

Psalm 103

Protecting Your Child from Sexual Predators

"Be on guard! Be alert! You do not know when that time will come. It's like a man going away: He leaves his house and puts his servants in charge, each with his assigned task, and tells the one at the door to keep watch." (Mark 13:33-34)

As we drove past the elementary school, we noticed the long line of cars waiting to pick up the children who were finishing their school day. "Boy," I commented—half speaking to my wife and half to myself—"things sure are different from when our kids went to school." A generation ago, perhaps even a decade ago, few parents had much concern when kids walked home. After all, there were neighbors and it was generally safe.

Today, it's a different world. Sexual predators know where to find kids, and a youngster with a lunch box or a backpack walking by himself becomes an unsuspecting target, a potential victim. Dangers far more deadly than nerve gas or chemical warfare lurk out there as predators target our children with sexual violence.

How do you protect your child from sexual predators? How do you warn your kids that everybody can't be trusted while you emphasize family solidarity and respect for elders? It's not easy, but if you don't teach your child to be alert and perceptive, it can be the gravest mistake you ever make. In some cases, a parent's negligence can be fatal; in others, a parent's failure results in emotional scars to a child that are there for life.

Step #1: Know who is apt to take advantage of your child.

The most likely predator is not the notorious ex-con who has just been released from prison. It's someone you and probably your child already know. The fact is that eighty percent of all sexual predators are acquaintances or friends of the family, and that fact in itself disarms the youngster, who reasons, "How could this nice person—daddy's friend, Uncle Paul or Grandpa—do something bad?" He's apt to be a nice guy—a stepdad, a distant relative, a scoutmaster who likes sleepovers with the boys or—as sad and inappropriate as it is—the youth pastor or the parish priest.

> *If you simply choose to look the other way or allow denial out of embarrassment, you may well contribute to ongoing abuse.*

Step #2: Educate, teach and instruct.

Make sure your children know what's proper and improper: that it's OK for a family member or close friend to touch a shoulder but not any part of the body that would be covered by a swimsuit.

Step #3: Be perceptive without being paranoid.

This is for both you and your child. Many children become victims when a stranger asks for help or someone shows up and says, "Your mom wants me to take you home," when you are the one who normally picks up your child. In a non-frightening but firm manner, you must teach your youngster that if someone tries to grab him, bite, yell and scream, run—but don't get in the car and go with the stranger.

Step #4: Know the symptoms of abuse.

In an article entitled, "Sudden Mood Swings Called Clues to Abuse," Carolyn Poirot, a writer for the *Fort Worth Star-Telegram*, says, "If children have been sexually abused outside the home, they may not want to go to school or the day care center and may cry and cling to mother. Or they regress."[10]

> ## Insight
>
> *Our hesitance to talk about sex or to insure our small children know their phone numbers and how to call 911 helps make it easy for sexual predators to take advantage of our children.*

Step #5: Never give anyone a second chance.

Forgiveness is not the issue; the safety of your child is. In all probability your youngster is not a sexual predator's first victim. If you simply choose to look the other way or allow denial out of embarrassment, you may well contribute to ongoing abuse.

Step #6: Always believe your child when he tells you about inappropriate activity.

Your child has no cause to deceive you. Children rarely lie about these matters.

Step #7: Realize there is healing and help if you have been a victim.

This applies not only to your child but to you as well. The dark sin we thought wasn't there a generation ago *was* there. And for you, who were victims long ago, there is healing and help. But God forbid that by indifference or neglect we should make it easy for anyone to be a sexual predator.

Think on This

1. Make sure your children know they should tell you if someone takes advantage of them.
2. Work out a backup plan—what to do if you should be delayed in traffic, who they can trust if you should go home from the office sick and couldn't pick them up.
3. Be alert. If your baby-sitter wants to bring her boyfriend to help her, it's better to cancel your evening than run the risk of someone taking advantage of your one-year-old who can't talk.

Resource Reading
2 Timothy 3:1-9

ωinning the Battle over Values

"Eli asked, 'What happened, my son?' " (1 Samuel 4:16)

arenting is one of the scariest things that a person ever does in his lifetime. Walk a tightrope over Niagara Falls, free fall out of an airplane, climb Mt. Everest or hang glide over Tokyo and you are apt to walk away from it. But this business of parenting can do you in for sure. It comes with no guarantees, and there is no customer service center where you can exchange a kid and start over.

Even Christian leaders—godly men and women—can be failures when it comes to raising children. And when that happens, we tend to think, *If they can't get the job done, what makes me think I can?*

There are the parents like Jonathan Edwards, whose godly descendants number among the hundreds, including Christian doctors, lawyers, judges and educators. Then there are those like Hannah Whitall Smith, a godly woman and author, whose children all grew up and turned their backs on God and Christian values. *If someone like that was a failure as a parent,* we think, *then how can I succeed as a parent in today's world of drugs, promiscuity and tremendous peer pressure?* I'm glad you asked, because today's guideline answers that very issue.

What can parents do to win at parenting?

Guideline #1: Keep your relationships right with God and your mate.

Nothing is more important than standing together spiritually as a husband and wife. Remember, values are caught, not taught. When two parents love each other, support each other, pray together and go to church together, they have a hedge against future failure that can come no other way. Does this mean that a single parent can't raise godly children? Not for a minute, but when one parent teaches one set of values, and the other teaches the opposite, the challenge of successful parenting is far greater.

You are your child's most effective teacher.

Guideline #2: Protect your child's environment.

A farmer was talking about raising chickens when he said, "You don't put live chicks under a dead hen." Neither do you expose your child to spiritually devastating influences and expect them to come through unscathed. Christian parents need to take seriously the teaching of Scripture that contends we are in the world but not of the world.

The battle lines are drawn today, and to ignore that fact exposes your child to a host of things that will leave their mark on his life and soul. At some point you've got to be willing to draw the line and say, "This far, and not an inch farther."

Environment includes what comes into your home through television, what your children are exposed to in a classroom, your children's friends. A whole gamut of important issues are raised: Should I put my children in private school, home school or take my chances in public school? There is no easy answer, but the issue of environment must be faced.

Guideline #3: Teach your child to think for himself and to evaluate what he hears and sees.

In recent days I have become absolutely convinced that teaching a child to think through cause-and-effect relationships gives him the strength to say, "No way! I choose to be my own person."

Guideline #4: Model the message yourself.

You are your child's most effective teacher. "Do not be deceived: God cannot be mocked," says Paul. "A man reaps what he sows. The one who sows to please his sinful nature, from that nature will reap destruction; the one who sows to please the Spirit, from the Spirit will reap eternal life" (Galatians 6:7-8). It is still true of parenting today.

Insight

The guidelines in this selection seem like a big order. The way to accomplish that is to take life one day at a time, one problem at a time, one question at a time. Someone said, "Inch by inch, life's a cinch; yard by yard, life is hard." It's also true of parenting.

Think on This

1. The force of peers can be lessened only by bringing new friends into the life of your child, ones who have the same set of values you have and are committed to what you believe is important. Where do you find these? Your church? Your family and close friends?

2. Two extremes are wrong—being too strict (withdrawn and separated from what you feel is wrong) and too permissive (anything goes). Where do you find yourself? How do you find balance?

3. When you and your mate disagree, how do you handle it?

Resource Reading

1 Samuel 4

Passing the Baton

*"So now, if the boy is not with us when I go back to
your servant my father and if my father, whose life is
closely bound up with the boy's life, sees that the boy
isn't there, he will die." (Genesis 44:30-31)*

When Olympic games are on the horizon, thousands of athletes from all over the world engage in serious training. Almost every Olympics brings new world records and a new class of hero-athletes. The margin of success is often so narrow—even a fraction of a second—that one slight mistake can mean disaster.

In the relay events, an athlete must run alongside the next runner and slap the baton into his open hand. Then he accelerates and runs until it is his turn to pass the baton to the next person.

In the summer Olympics of 1996, one national relay team was expected to win or at least place among the medalists, but their hopes were dashed when the lead runner reached for the open hand of his successor, who grasped the baton, then dropped it. By the time he had recovered the baton, the race was history and his team had lost. I still remember the time and the place where I watched Zola Budd running barefoot in the Olympics of 1984 as Mary Decker tripped over her and both stumbled badly.

Frankly, I like to win. Of course, winning isn't everything, but there is no thrill comparable to being the first to break the tape or to come in ahead of your competitor, even if it is by a hair. I'm the same way when it comes to parenting. No parent who really loves his children wants to see a single one stumble and fall.

How does a parent pass the baton of faith, slapping it into the hands of the next generation, who grasp it and begin to convey the same value system that they received growing up? Those who do succeed have a reward far greater than standing on the winner's pedestal and having a gold medallion placed around their neck.

You can't pass the baton of faith to your offspring unless you have it firmly in your grasp yourself.

That's where a lot of parents fail. "Don't do as I do," they tell their kids. "You do as I say." Forget it. You can lecture your kids on right and wrong until you have calluses on your vocal chords and wind erosion on your teeth, and it is a waste of your breath unless you live the life before them. If you want a winner, then preach less and practice more.

> *If you want a winner, then preach less and practice more.*

Giving your child a lively and virile faith in God, a knowledge of right and wrong and an understanding of fairness and compassion is placing the baton of faith firmly in the grasp of your offspring. They may stumble, but chances are they will never lose the grasp on what you have given them.

Model the value system that you believe is important.

Winning is important, but winning isn't as important as striving fairly and honestly. Ben Johnson, known as "the human bullet," often described as "the fastest man alive," learned this the hard way. Though he won his event, he was later disqualified for taking steroids in the summer Olympics of 1988. Surrendering his medal with disgrace, he returned to his homeland in Canada a subdued man.

Be there when your son or daughter needs your help.

Who will forget the image of the dad in the summer Olympics of 1992 whose son pulled a hamstring? As the dad ran out on the track he put his arms under his son and the two of them limped toward the finish line. While most of us have forgotten his name, none who saw it will ever forget the emotional impact of a dad who was there.

> *Insight*
>
> *Every parent, no matter what he does—either negatively or positively—is conveying a message to his child regarding values, regarding right and wrong, regarding God and our world.*

To pass the baton of faith to your offspring, love your children unconditionally and keep the lines of communication open.

A dad doesn't reject his little boy who stumbles and falls learning to walk, just as a wise father doesn't disown the teenage son who is learning through failure.

Someone once said that your children are the only thing you can take to heaven with you. As Judah put it long ago, "How can I go back to my father if the boy is not with me?" (Genesis 44:34). Yes, how?

Think on This

1. If you can't give your children faith because you don't have it yourself, get on your knees and ask God to forgive you, to give you strength to live for Him and to be the best mom or dad you can be.
2. The impact of a changed life as you turn the corner with God and begin to walk with Him speaks louder to your child than your previous failures.

Resource Reading

Genesis 44

Because I Said So

*"Children, obey your parents in everything,
for this pleases the Lord." (Colossians 3:20)*

A child doesn't want to clean up the vegetables on his plate, and though he has asked the question a million—maybe 2 million times—he asks it anyway. He knows it is always good for a few more seconds of stalling: "Why do I have to eat my vegetables?"

The parent, however, has just seen the needle on his patience meter hit the top—the red part which indicates a very explosive situation. In this danger zone, parents are liable to all kinds of unbecoming thoughts and acts. They are prone to use words which should not be used in front of little children.

Who knows what might happen? But then, the parent, remembering all the good books about parenting and keeping his temper and how important it is to provide a role model for his child, bites his lip until it is almost ready to bleed, clenches his teeth and says, "BECAUSE I SAID SO!" Those words are always spoken in capital letters followed by an exclamation point which is still smoking when it sizzles across the teeth.

That line has been used for centuries! It is what you always say when you have exhausted your patience and you no longer trust yourself not to become violent. So you, having heard those words when you were a child, pass on that line to your own child: "BECAUSE I SAID SO!" Hearing those words, a child realizes that he has lost the battle, that dialogue has irretrievably broken down, and he had better cultivate a taste for vegetables—fast. Discussion ended.

A slightly more civilized, cultured version was the wording on a sweatshirt worn by a young mother who was pushing a double-seated baby stroller, one of those affairs that will hold two children plus a couple duffel bags of diapers and bottles. The slogan read, "Because I'm the Mommy—That's Why!"

Now, frankly, as a grandfather who is presently enjoying watching an eighteen-month-old assert his independence just as his mother did some thirty years ago, I understand this whole issue. At some point—preferably very early in the parenting process—parents must learn an important lesson: *Parenting is the raising of children by parents, not the raising of parents by children.*

Somebody is going to be in charge, and it had better be Mommy and Daddy, as God so ordered, or else for the next eighteen years, you are in for a very rough ride.

> *Parenting is the raising of children by parents, not the raising of parents by children.*

Raising your voice to the level whereby crystal could be broken and saying, "BECAUSE I SAID SO!" is overkill. Establishing parental authority is not a matter of noise or decibels, but it does involve saying what you mean and meaning what you say. This can be done lovingly, quietly, and shouldn't have to be very often said or done. But the message should come through: "I'm the parent and that settles the issue." And why should you accept what I've just said? "BECAUSE I SAID SO—THAT'S WHY!"

Think on This

Insight

Leadership—the quiet kind which God wants you to exert in your family—is not a matter of being a bully, a dictator or a boss. It is simply taking control and doing the right thing.

1. Providing an alternative or a choice of two things—both of which are acceptable to you—may help involve your child in decision-making.

2. When you speak kindly but firmly it saves having to raise your voice several decibels before your child knows that you really mean business.

3. Asking your child to stop what he is doing and look at you as you ask for something to be done focuses attention and eliminates the possibility that you are not being heard.

Resource Reading

Colossians 3

Raising Positive Kids in a Negative World

*"The LORD called Samuel a third time, and Samuel got
up and went to Eli and said, 'Here I am; you called me.'
Then Eli realized that the LORD was calling the boy."*
(1 Samuel 3:8)

In his book *Raising Positive Kids in a Negative World*, Zig
Zigler says that the key to successful parenting isn't
what parents do, but *what they are*.[11] Zigler is right. "The
kid's a chip off the old block," we sometimes say of a
youngster who resembles his dad. Or we say, "Like father,
like son." Raising positive kids in a negative world begins
in your heart, not your vocal chords. It's what you are, not
what you say, that counts the most. It's your model that
most influences your children.

Anyone who runs a long race always looks back and reflects
on the path he just took on. He remembers the rough spots,
the challenges that could have caused failure. Parents do the
same thing, and it doesn't just happen when you walk your
daughter down the aisle. It's for a lifetime.

In my file are more letters than I can count from parents
who look back and ask, "Where did I go wrong?" In many
cases it was not the parent who went wrong. It was a youth
who chose to walk a different path.

Compiling the selections for this book has given me a new focus on the process of parenting, both as a dad and grandfather, and as a friend and counselor to a lot of people.

I often see two sets of parents raising their children in the same basic environment and culture. Yet one set of kids goes straight and makes their parents proud, and other kids get derailed, often mortgaging their futures and blighting their hope of getting anywhere in life. What's the difference?

I'm convinced that one powerful factor is how parents help their children think of themselves, which, in turn, gives their kids enough strength to stand alone when they need to, to have the strength to walk away from bad situations and withstand negative peer pressures. If, of course, I could produce a vitamin or a serum which would produce this kind of behavior, I could retire immediately. But if such a thing were ever invented, we would lose the challenge and the thrill of growing positive kids in a negative world.

One powerful factor in raising positive kids is how parents help their children to think of themselves, which gives their kids enough strength to stand alone when they need to.

I am convinced that three ingredients go into the formula of producing positive kids in a negative world.

1. Self-esteem

The first factor is self-esteem, or an understanding of who a child is in relationship to parents, God and family. This involves handling failures, knowing how to be independent and having the proper tension between living relevant lives and the pressures of conformity. It also means knowing what the distance between your home and the world should be.

2. Self-assurance

The world is no friend to your children. It's tough out there. It's not only the neighborhood bully who is the enemy. Your child may also fight racial prejudice, poor education and training and a host of other factors. He needs a faith in God and himself which becomes an anchor.

Insight

Attitudes are catching! When you are convinced that your youngster can do something and can convey that quiet confidence, it helps him to step out and eventually succeed.

3. Motivation

You need to decide what road your child will travel long before he knows. Proverbs 22:6 talks of the path that a child should go, but you must first make that choice. This is also where God's will comes into the picture, and you must grasp that truth and help guide your youngster morally and spiritually.

Raising positive, godly kids in a negative, ungodly world is one of the greatest accomplishments of life. Your task and your accomplishment are far greater than the world knows. But God knows, and you will have His help as you do your part.[12]

Think on This

1. Be discerning in what you ask of a child. Obviously, a four-year-old can't hit a ball like an eight-year-old brother because there is a physical limitation.

2. Understand that girls are better at verbal tasks, boys better at physical tasks. That's how God made us. Don't try to put them into the same mold. Girls also mature faster than boys do. Know what your child is capable of doing. Make sure you validate him with praise and encouragement, not censure and ridicule over failure.

Resource Reading
Psalm 37:1-7

Growing a Kid So Strong He Won't Need You

*"Only be careful, and watch yourselves closely so that
you do not forget the things your eyes have seen or
let them slip from your heart as long as you live.
Teach them to your children and to their
children after them." (Deuteronomy 4:9)*

There comes a time in the life of every teenager when he can do whatever he wants because he's beyond the reach of Mom or Dad. How do you grow a kid so strong that he won't need you when you aren't there? That should be the goal of every parent, and there aren't many years in which to lay that kind of a foundation. I call it giving your child the gift of self-reliance.

There is little need for me to tell you that it's tough to be successful when it comes to this business of parenting. The media, the pressure of other teens and the number of ways there are to go wrong when there is only one way to go right make it tough on teens as well. The pressure to go along, to be like everybody else, to push aside what Mom and Dad say—to just "do it"—is very, very powerful. In recent days I've asked myself what it takes to produce self-reliance in teens, to help them be strong enough, self-confident enough that they can distance themselves from what they know is wrong. This, of course, is the challenge.

I'm convinced that three powerful factors contribute to producing personal strength in the life of a teenager, and the absence of these qualities in the lives of so many today explains the number of teenage pregnancies, the rise of gangs, the unprecedented incidence of the use of drugs. What are these factors that produce the strength to say *no* with conviction?

Factor #1: Family identity

This is probably the most important factor of all. The presence of a dad in a family unit along with family cohesiveness is itself a foundation for personal strength. I happen to believe that since God designed conception in such a way that two persons—a mother and a father—are necessary to bring a child into the world, He intended both to participate in the process of teaching and raising a child.

Values are established from within the family, and kids grow up with them.

Today there are two basic kinds of families, contend Gary and Ann Marie Ezzo, founders of the ministry Growing Kids God's Way—the interdependent family and the independent family. In the former family unit, the extended family is important. Traditions, family meals, grandparents, family outings all are important. Values are established from within the family, and kids grow up with them. Kids are expected to be there for meals, to participate in family discussions, to conform to the values established by parents. Loyalty, teamwork and commitment are not optional. They are expected.

In contrast, the independent family finds significance through relationships outside the family unit. Values and worth come from peers, not parents. Self-expression is the norm, and the individual is emphasized.

Factor #2: An independence from the culture and the world that surrounds them

Does this mean teens should be recluses, disconnected from the world? No, but they build an ego and self-image strong enough that their self-worth is not derived from the culture and the world surrounding them. They are OK, and they know it. They don't have to "go along" to "get along."

Factor #3: A sense of value and self-worth which helps them understand their true importance

> ## Insight
> *Children are going to derive their sense of value and self-worth from the individuals and culture that surround them—playmates, caregivers, friends, parents and relatives. Lot's daughters were negatively influenced by the city in which they lived and the wicked people who lived there. Putting distance between you and evil is not only prudent but is essential in raising godly kids.*

It is here that faith in God and an understanding of their true worth in God's sight and in the minds of their parents are positive forces for good.

You *can* grow a youngster so strong that he doesn't need you. Long ago God instructed, "Train a child in the way he should go, and when he is old he will not turn from it" (Proverbs 22:6), and I would add, "And you will be glad you did!"[13]

Think on This

1. Who was a significant influence in your life as a child? Why and how did this person influence you?
2. Which means more to your children—members of the family (including brothers, sisters and cousins) or outside friends?
3. Of those outside friends, how many of them are from families holding the same values as you?

Resource Reading

Genesis 19

Growing Kids God's Way

*"Sons are a heritage from the LORD, children a
reward from him. Like arrows in the hands of a warrior
are sons born in one's youth." (Psalm 127:3-4)*

When you love your children, there are six gifts
which you should give them—gifts which cost
nothing in terms of money but are very costly in the currency
of time, energy and emotion. Incidentally, all of these six are
important when it comes to successful parenting or growing
kids God's way.

Gift #1 is the gift of yourself.

Some parents give almost everything to their kids but the
gift of themselves. Their kids have the latest in clothes, TVs,
Nintendo games, DVDs, CDs and Walkmans—all kinds of
things, but lack the mom or dad. The gift of yourself is really
the gift of love.

My friend, Dr. Ross Campbell, psychiatrist and author of
the book *How to Really Love Your Child,* says that he has never
treated an adolescent involved in sexual misconduct who felt
really loved by parents. Stop long enough for a reality check:
How much of yourself do you give to the child you brought
into the world?

Gift #2 is the gift of self-esteem.

When a little boy about five years of age went out to dinner with his parents and the waiter took his order along with those of his parents, the little boy later commented, "Gee, Dad, he thinks I'm a real person!"

Everything you do affects the emotional strength of your child.

Very early in life we learn self-esteem or self-depreciation. "What a pretty baby you are!" or "What pretty eyes you have!" can later turn into, "How come you got a B- on your report card?" overlooking the five A's that are there. Build self-esteem in your child by:

- avoiding comparisons with other kids.
- telling your youngster how proud you are of him when he does well.
- accepting him just the same in a failure situation as you would in a success.
- being patient and having realistic expectations.
- realizing that every youngster matures at a different rate.

Gift #3 is the gift of self-reliance.

Your goal as a parent should be to grow a kid so strong that when you aren't there, he won't need you! "Just say no!" kids are told when their hormones and their peers say, "Why not?" Frankly, your child will have about the same emotional strength as does your family. Remember, he's the product of you who are his parents, and when you are strong emotionally, you pass that strength on to him.

Realize that everything you do affects the emotional strength of your child. One of the greatest gifts you can give your child is to love your spouse. This puts to rest one of the greatest fears of kids today—the fear that Mommy and Daddy may not stay together.

Gift #4 is the gift of discerning value versus worth.

Offer a four-year-old a bright red toy car or a crisp new $100 bill. Which will he take? Obviously, the bright toy. But as he grows older he's got to learn the difference between satisfying his biological urges and realizing the cost, in terms of life, which his decision may bring.

Gift #5 is the gift of self-discipline.

Psychologists have discovered that children who can defer gratification become stronger and more productive as adults. They will place one marshmallow in front of a child and say, "You may have this now, but if you wait until I run an errand and come back, you may have two." Kids who have the strength to wait develop self-discipline that makes a difference in life.

> ### Insight
>
> *All the expensive gifts in the world cannot replace the gift of yourself—your time, your love, your care, your thoughts, your touch, your compassion and your experiences.*

Gift #6 is the gift of faith in God.

This is a gift which you cannot give unless you possess it yourself. Though it isn't passed on through a genetic code, the baton of faith is passed from hand to hand when parents live what they talk and practice what they believe.

How many of these gifts have you given your child?[14]

Think on This

1. Make a list of the last five gifts you have given to your children.
2. Now make a list of the significant times you have been together as opposed to your child's doing things with peer group acquaintances. Which is the longer list?

Resource Reading

Colossians 3:12-21

Raising G-rated Kids in an X-rated World

"The righteous man leads a blameless life;
blessed are his children after him." (Proverbs 20:7)

Can you raise G-rated kids in an X-rated world? You bet you can, but it isn't easy. It's the challenge of the century, and certainly the challenge of your life. The following are five guidelines which can help you accomplish your goal.

Guideline #1: Set the example.

God made you the mommy or daddy, so assume your responsibility. You gave birth to a child. No one in the world—not your school or even your church—can as effectively provide a framework for integrity and character as can you. You are the one who can raise a G-rated kid in an X-rated world, one filled with moral and spiritual pollution.

If you are an R- or an X-rated parent, don't expect yours to be G-rated kids. You set the example. They learn from you. Never deceive yourself by telling your kids, "Don't do as I do; do as I say." Save your breath. What you do, they will do, but they will go one step beyond you—always.

Guideline #2: Help your child be his own person.

One of the greatest things you as parent can do for your child is to help him throw off the cookie-cutter, be-just-like-everyone-else mentality so prevalent today. This requires your putting a certain amount of space between your kids and the world, whose values are far from G-rated. It means you help your offspring to understand, "I don't have to be just like everybody else. It's OK to be me and to be different."

Your kids are going to hear and see a lot of junk outside your home, but having a standard at home says clearly, "We don't approve of that stuff, and we won't allow it in our home. We love you too much to let you warp your character with junk." Kids know the difference.

> *You have got to concentrate on feeding the moral and spiritual nature of your child.*

Guideline #3: Build character through the moral feeding and nurturing of your children.

I can tell you a thousand places where your children will not build character, including most movies, TV and the lyrics of a lot of contemporary music. You have got to concentrate on feeding the moral and spiritual nature of your child. This means Sunday school and church, youth activities, events and activities that are family-centered.

Sure, this inconveniences you as an adult. You've got to shut off the TV and pack the van and think about where you are going and what you are going to do. It means you monitor what comes into your home and what goes into the minds of your kids. This includes not only what you put on the table but the music that goes into the Walkman your teen listens to.

Guideline #4: Reinforce character with a positive peer group.

This means making it easy for your kids to be with others whose values are the same as yours and difficult to be with other kids who are being raised in a permissive environment without convictions. When you fail to make some decisions, by default you lose your influence for good and God.

Guideline #5: Empower your child with validation.

The most important thing in the life of a youngster isn't really, "What do my peers think of me?" in spite of the fact that we've bought into that mentality and touted it for a generation. The truth is that parental approval—hearing a dad say, "I'm really proud of you," or a mom say, "Sweetheart, you really handled that situation well. I couldn't have done better myself "—is the most meaningful validation in your kids' lives.

Insight

Remember, if you live in an R-rated world and think your children will live in a G-rated world, you're wrong! It's only a matter of time until they move quickly into your level, and—be sure of this—once they become teens they will go beyond your level. They won't stop where you draw the line.

You can raise G-rated kids in an X-rated world with God's help and a lot of dogged persistence. It's worth it. It will count and make a difference in tomorrow's world.

Think on This

1. Make sure you know what tapes or CDs your youngsters are listening to.
2. Take time to analyze the words and lyrics of songs.
3. Make sure you know something about the movies your kids go to see when you are not with them.
4. You protect your kids from viruses, from predators, from evil. Protect their minds from the evils that seduce them through the media.
5. If you deny your youngster something—"That's not good for you!"—replace it with something positive, something better. It's worth the cost. It's an investment in character and integrity.

Resource Reading

Proverbs 10:1-9

Cult Insurance

*"There is a way that seems right to a man,
but in the end it leads to death." (Proverbs 16:25)*

"Dear Dr. Sala," writes a friend, "what can I do to ensure that my kids will never become involved in a cult group?" There are some very positive things that you as a parent can do to ensure that your children will follow the Lord and won't be entangled in a cult group.

1. Help your child or teen to develop a warm, personal relationship with Jesus Christ.

I sincerely believe that it is right here where many parents fail, and the incipient seeds of failure burst forth in vulnerability. It is one thing to know about Christ; it is totally another thing for a young person to have a personal relationship with Him and to know how to sustain that relationship through prayer, the Word of God and fellowship with others in a peer group.

In Greek are two words which are usually translated "knowledge." The first word, *gnosis*, often implies head or theoretical knowledge, while the second word, *epignosis*, which is a compound of a preposition and the original word, means full or complete knowledge. To have the knowledge of Christ in your head is one thing; to have it in your heart is another. A lot of youngsters today have confused churchianity with

Christianity—the former means a social relationship; the latter a vital, personal relationship.

2. Help your child to know how to defend and substantiate what he believes.

To ensure that your youngster doesn't become involved in a cult group, give him a standard of measurement of biblical truth by which he can evaluate any group or teaching. Scores of people have become involved in cult groups thinking they were really studying the Bible and following the Lord. They simply didn't know the difference.

> *To have the knowledge of Christ in your head is one thing; to have it in your heart is another.*

A person has to know what a meter is before he can determine if a three-foot yardstick falls short. When it comes to spiritual truths, I've come to the conclusion that very, very few churches are able to do much in laying a foundation in the lives of young people. If you are not convinced, ask a group of high schoolers in your church what they believe and listen carefully. If, however, you asked a young follower of Hare Krishna what he believes, he can tell you every detail of his beliefs.

3. Know what your teenagers are thinking.

Remember, that's a good deal different from knowing what they are saying! Sandy Larsen, who with her husband has developed a ministry counseling with young people involved in cults, contends that church-related young people are often programmed in such a manner that they come up with right answers, answers that they really question deep in their hearts. But parents, Sunday school teachers or youth workers feel challenged by their questions, and subsequently kids avoid their reactions by *saying* the right things—but not really believing them.

How do you find out what teens are thinking? Mostly by listening. A few penetrating questions will often prime the pump. Keep in mind, though, that if you come down like a ton of bricks on your teenager every time he says something that isn't quite right on target, there isn't much hope of ever learning what he is really thinking.

4. Provide the warm supportive environment in your home that cancels out the psychological appeal and support of a cult group.

I'm quick to recognize that some parents have had close-knit, warm relationships with their kids and their children still became involved in cult groups. Yet the fact remains that many, if not most, of the young people involved in cult groups are

Insight

Generally (though certainly not always), the attraction of a cult comes through the affirmation, acceptance and strength of a group, which is often lacking in a family, especially a dysfunctional family. Your personal family is strengthened by the bonds to a church family.

from broken homes or homes where there is little family cohesiveness. Unfortunately the cult group becomes the family a youngster never had. Following the guidelines I've outlined in this selection will keep you from someday saying, "What happened? How did my kid fall for their line?"

Think on This

1. If you have teens or preteens who are really dissatisfied with your church (even though your family has been there for years), better check out some other churches. Having kids involved in church in their teen years is important.
2. When your youngster is invited to join a youth group that's having a conference, make sure you know who is sponsoring it, what they believe and who is in charge. You could be exposing your youngster to grave danger.
3. Remember, knowing what you believe is prerequisite to teaching your children what to believe. You've got to know what a straight line is before you know what a crooked one is.
4. Not all religions lead to God. Jesus said, "I am the way and the truth and the life. No one comes to the Father except through me" (John 14:6). It's OK to be as narrow as Scripture.

Resource Reading

Galatians 5-6

Drawing the Line

*"Cast your bread upon the waters, for after many
days you will find it again." (Ecclesiastes 11:1)*

Wise is the parent who draws a line and says, "This far and no farther. The line is not negotiable, and I will not give in to your yelling and screaming." We parents are human. We like to make our kids happy, and we certainly don't relish arguments with our small fry. But in a culture where almost anything goes and our kids' argument, "Everybody else gets to do it" is often valid, a loving, thoughtful parent has to draw the line.

No matter where you draw the line, your youngster will push for a bit more. That's human nature. Go to the largest cattle ranch in the world and cross miles of prairie and sagebrush, and there you will find a cow with its head stuck through the barbed-wire fence trying to nibble on the grass just beyond its reach. That's human nature as well.

A dad, concerned that his four youngsters would get hurt playing in the street in front of their house, drew a chalk line on the pavement and said, "OK, you can play in the street, but stay on this side of the chalk line." When he came home that night—you guessed it—he found his four kids standing on the chalk line.

Many parents didn't draw lines for their kids, and their grown children are paying the price. They are struggling because they didn't believe they had to show up at work on time, live within the law or drive without drinking.

The fact is that life draws lines that are hard and nonnegotiable. When you ignore them, you suffer the consequences. When a parent fails to draws lines, it's like trying to play a game with no rules. Sooner or later, there are consequences—severe ones too.

> *Drawing lines and lovingly enforcing them helps prepare a kid for life.*

Drawing lines and lovingly enforcing them helps prepare a kid for life. It also makes it easier for him as he grows up. How? First, it takes the pressure off of him with his peers. He can grouch and say, "I can't do that! My mom won't let me," making you the bad guy, but he doesn't end up in a situation he would prefer to avoid but doesn't know how to.

It also brings peace to your home. There's an 11 o'clock curfew on Friday and Saturday nights, and unless something very, very big comes up, that's the way it is, thus preventing arguments.

Drawing lines and staying within the boundaries also teaches a spiritual lesson. God draws lines too, and though there is forgiveness with Him, we still reap the consequences of our failures when we ignore His boundaries. Galatians 6:7 says, "Don't be misled; remember that you can't ignore God and get away with it: a man will always reap just the kind of crop he sows!" (TLB).

Knowing what the boundaries are—whether they are yours or God's—brings security. You know when you are within the framework of acceptable behavior and when you have gone beyond the pale of safety.

Wise is the parent who loves enough, cares enough and is strong enough to say, "I love you too much to let you do anything you want!" and quietly draws a line, saying, "This is as far as you can go!"

Eventually your son or daughter will grow up and say, "Thanks, Mom, thanks, Dad. I'm glad you cared enough to draw a line."

Insight

Boundaries provide security from without and within. Knowing that you are within the boundary takes the pressure off and provides peace of mind for you as a parent and for your child as well. Having a boundary is also like a fence that keeps encroachments out.

Think on This

1. Some boundaries are nonnegotiable. They are fixed and not subject to discussion. Some, however, may need flexibility on occasion.

2. A youngster should have the right to express himself and voice dissent in an agreeable fashion, but he also needs to be willing (once an issue has been heard fairly) to accept the decision of a parent.

3. Listening is important. If your child knows that he has had a fair hearing, he will be more apt to accept the boundaries you lay down than if he feels that his feelings and thoughts don't count.

Resource Reading

Genesis 27

The Triumph of Tough Love

*"How great is the love the Father has lavished on us,
that we should be called children of God! And that is
what we are! The reason the world does not know us
is that it did not know him. Dear friends, now we
are the children of God, and what we will be has
not yet been made known. But we know that when
he appears, we shall be like him, for we shall see
him as he is." (1 John 3:1-2)*

Have you as a parent ever felt like giving up on a teenager when he turned his back on you and God and went the route of the Prodigal? Then this selection is just for you. As you can see, I've called it The Triumph of Tough Love. Now here's the question that launches our discussion: Is it possible for you as parent to separate your youngster's behavior from your acceptance of him?

Not only is it possible, it is absolutely necessary. Sooner or later almost every parent has to say, "Look, kid, I love you, but what you are doing doesn't make the grade—I detest it." You reject the behavior, not the person.

That is the opposite of what one dad did. When his son started smoking pot, the father, who had raised his three boys with rigid discipline, said, "You either get rid of that stuff or you get out of the house."

Ultimatums are dangerous. When you say, "You do this, or else . . . ," you are drawing a line and saying, "I dare you to step over it." An ultimatum to a teen or a young adult who considers himself to be very mature (when in reality he is rather immature) is like waving a flag in front of a bull. In defiance he rears back and says, "Oh yeah—just try me."

You've probably guessed what happened. The youngster left home. With no place to go, he started sleeping in the backseats of parked automobiles until the police found him. It was either go to jail or get off the street. With no place to go and no money, he went back to the pusher and started selling marijuana. In short order he had graduated to heroin, and by the time the dad realized what a tragic mistake he had made, the boy had become addicted.

> To get revenge on our children for hurting our family pride, we step on them when they need our help the most.

There are times when the situation requires of you the loving action of saying, "This is it. You need help and I'm going to see that you get it." That's tough love. You don't want to, but you have to for the sake of the other children in your family. However, before you say, "You do this or else," think and pray about the implications and see if there is a better way to handle the situation.

Unconditional love, the tough kind God has for us and the kind we must have for each other in the family, means acceptance, but it also separates behavior from acceptance. Another thing about unconditional love is that it embraces forgiveness and finally leads to self-acceptance and assurance. It's a package and the last two characteristics are tremendously important.

Paul wrote, "Be ye kind one to another, tenderhearted, forgiving one another, even as God for Christ's sake hath forgiven you" (Ephesians 4:32, KJV). The model of God's tough love that encompasses forgiveness was the Father's love for us. Forgiveness isn't something you earn or deserve; it's something freely extended as the result of the kindness of your heart.

You don't deserve God's forgiveness any more than your child deserves to be forgiven when he has fallen on his face. Sometimes we parents do what no animal would ever do: shoot our own flesh and blood—our kids who have been taken captive by the lusts of the world. Often we do so because our pride has taken a hit, our image has been tarnished, we've been embarrassed by the things our kids have done. To get our revenge, we step on them when they need our help the most.

To love without having the love returned demands the unconditional love which God has for us. Paul spoke of it, saying, "God demonstrates his own love for us in this: While we were still sinners, Christ died for us" (Romans 5:8). As Charles Wesley put it, "Died He for me, who caused His

> ## Insight
>
> *Looking beyond the immediate problem—the situation that distresses—to the future helps you see the larger picture. The immediate crisis will pass, but what you do now may determine whether or not you will be part of the future of your teenager. Don't burn your bridges.*

pain, for me, who Him, to death pursued? Amazing love! How can it be that Thou, my God, shoudst die for me?"

Think on This

1. You've got to decide where to draw the line. But remember, once you draw the line and pronounce the ultimatum, "You do this or else!" you had better be willing to live with the "or else!" because that's probably what is going to happen.
2. Before you pronounce an ultimatum, do three things:
   - Make the situation a sustained matter of prayer.
   - Talk over the situation with a friend and make sure you and your spouse are together in what you decide, and
   - Be willing to live with the consequences of your decision.

Resource Reading

1 Corinthians 13 (I suggest that you read this passage every day this week. It's life-changing!)

Should You Beat 'Em Now and Then to Keep 'Em in Line?

"Do not withhold discipline from a child; if you punish him with the rod, he will not die." (Proverbs 23:13)

When I was guest professor at Donetsk Christian University in the Ukraine, I taught a family living section for college students who had come from all over the former USSR. When I asked them to write a family history, a large percentage of the students—if not the majority—told about being beaten or severely punished as children. One young man told me that when he was growing up in Moscow, it was accepted practice for parents to beat their children periodically. He said his parents actually believed that whether or not a child had misbehaved, occasionally thrashing a child was good for him.

Dealing with the subject, I also learned something which impressed me in a negative way. The traditional Russian Bible has no word for discipline—only punishment. Subsequently, the idea of discipline as being opposed to punishment was something quite novel to these students.

Does the Bible differentiate between discipline and punishment? Yes, clearly it does. The New Testament word *paideuo*, usually translated "to discipline" in the New Testament, is much different from the word *paio*, which means "to strike, hit or wound." The latter word was used of Jesus Christ when He was scourged by the Roman soldiers. The former word, which also was translated "to instruct, train, correct or give guidance to," was used of a father's guidance of his son, or even an instructor's correction of a student.

When a child misbehaves, should he be punished or disciplined? Not simply splitting hairs over semantics, I must point out that there is a vast difference between the two. When a person commits a crime, people are incensed! They cry for justice. The focus is on the past—what happened. The general public isn't so much concerned about what this person does in the future as they are about his paying the price of his wrongdoing. That's punishment.

> *The whole concept of biblical discipline is to get the message across that what an individual has done is wrong, and in the future this kind of conduct just is not acceptable.*

But the issue of a child's needing correction is totally different. The point of focus is not what happened in the past that was wrong, but what is not going to be allowed in the future. The emotion generating punishment is anger, while the emotion prompting discipline is love.

The whole concept of biblical discipline is to get the message across that what an individual has done is wrong, and in the future this kind of conduct just is not acceptable. I freely concede the fact that some parents, not knowing the difference, do punish their children; but far wiser is the parent who knows the difference and learns that discipline is both necessary and effective.

No successful person ever makes it to the top without learning the value and importance of knowing how to discipline himself, a practice which needs to be learned early in life, and the earlier the better.

Discipline balanced with love is a winner. It is the sure enforcer of the learning process that produces well-adjusted individuals who are in control of themselves and will ultimately make their mark in the world.

Discipline begins with parents who are in con-

> ## Insight
>
> Knowing the difference between discipline and punishment gives parenting a completely different perspective.

trol and who convey the importance of that same quality to their kids. The Bible is clear that God disciplines those whom He loves, bringing us back to the path from which we have strayed, and the godly parent who loves his child and disciplines him in love is modeling this great truth.

May God deliver us from punishment, but may He give parents enough love to learn to discipline. There is a great difference between the two.

Think on This

This selection is the first that focuses on the importance of discipline. There are many ways you can provide discipline apart from physical discipline. Sit down at this point and make a list. Which of these is most effective? Should you use it in every situation?

Resource Reading

Proverbs 23

When Your Child Needs Discipline

"No discipline seems pleasant at the time, but painful. Later on, however, it produces a harvest of righteousness and peace for those who have been trained by it." (Hebrews 12:11)

Divide and conquer is not only the *modus operandi* of warfare, but it is also the strategy of kids who know that if they can play parents against each other, or pit weariness against the single parent, they have won the battle. Our English word "discipline" comes from the Latin word *discere*, which means "to know," or in the broader sense, "to discern."

Yet the fact remains that providing discipline for children is one of the most distasteful things in the whole spectrum of parenting. Regardless of how tired or stressed-out a parent may be, enforcing the teaching-learning process is one of the most important contributions a parent makes to the future of his children.

When a youngster's behavior deteriorates to the place where discipline is necessary, you need to ask some important questions.

"Why has discipline become an issue?"

Kids have an amazing radar system. When you are under stress, kids automatically pick up on that fact, but they don't understand the pressure you are under. They just sense that Mom or Dad is really edgy, and quite often their behavior is an attempt to get your attention. A child deprived of sleep is going to be fussy—that's not an issue which requires discipline. But an eight-year-old who tells his mother to shut up because he's talking on the telephone is a boy headed for real trouble as a teenager.

Almost always improper behavior is a red flag which says, "You need to spend more time with me!" Or, "I want your attention, and I want it so badly that I am willing to risk getting into trouble to get it."

L ife is a far sterner taskmaster than the parent who loves his child and insists that the youngster learns to do right!

"Have I made it clear that certain things are totally off-limits in our family, and that when those things are chosen, discipline is the result?"

A parent who takes out his anger on his child treats the youngster unfairly, but the parent who lets children know that some things aren't going to be allowed does his youngster a great favor: he is equipping the youngster for life—which is a far sterner taskmaster than the parent who loves his child and insists that the youngster learns to do right!

When behavior becomes a problem, you need to go one step further by asking—

"Am I consistent in what I expect?"

Let's say bedtime is 9 o'clock. But you aren't consistent about enforcing it. And then when you are crabby, you yell at your kids because it is after 10 and they still aren't in bed. You are sending conflicting messages, which create insecurity. Being consistent is tough, but it's important.

One little fellow knew that his dad meant what he said and said what he meant. After the little boy went to bed, he called out, "Daddy, can I have a drink of water?"

His father, who knew he was stalling, answered, "No, son, go to sleep."

Five minutes later came another plea, "Please, Daddy, can I have a drink of water?"

"No, son, and if you ask one more time, I'm going to spank you."

For five minutes there was absolute silence, and then a resigned little voice says, "Daddy, when you get up to spank me, can I have a glass of water?"

Finally, there is one more question.

> ## Insight
>
> *Being sensitive to the cause of a problem is a key to helping you deal with it wisely. For example, when a child is really tired, he's apt to fuss and annoy you. "You sit still and be quiet or I'm going to whip you!" Wrong. He doesn't need discipline; he needs sleep.*

"What is the best way to deal with this situation?"

How you do it has so much to do with its effectiveness. Anger creates anger, but discipline administered with love produces well-adjusted children who know the difference between right and wrong and choose to do right.

Well, the book of Hebrews says, "No discipline seems pleasant at the time, but painful. Later on, however, it produces a harvest of righteousness and peace for those who have been trained by it" (12:11). So be it.

Think on This

1. Disciplining a child for what he cannot help (say, a three-year-old who still wets the bed at night) produces anger and frustration. But willful disobedience and defiance are two situations that cannot be ignored. How do you know the difference?
2. Make sure that you clarify what is right and wrong—what is acceptable or unacceptable—before you discipline.
3. Take a Bible concordance and look up the word "discipline." Jot down each reference. Then read the verses, making notes of the benefits attached to correction.

Resource Reading
Hebrews 12:1-12

The Benefits of Discipline

"A wise son brings joy to his father, but a foolish son grief to his mother." (Proverbs 10:1)

Motivational speaker and storyteller Ethel Barrett tells of a time she was waiting her turn in a beauty shop. A little boy, about four years of age, started yelling and screaming at the top of his lungs. Most folks tried to ignore the unruly child, but then a gray-haired lady gruffly barked, "Sit down!" and the four-year-old, ready to do battle with her, threw a magazine at her.

Like a drill sergeant, she gave the order again, "Sit down!" and this time she picked him up and sat him in a chair. The little boy let out a blood-curdling scream which could be heard miles away. Picking up the magazine which had been thrown at her, she began to turn the pages, asking, "What's that?" pointing to the pictures. The little boy still paid no attention and yelled at the top of his lungs. The gray-haired grandmother kept turning the pages until the little boy had begun responding, naming the things in the pictures.

Finally, the grandmother wiped away his tears, and he was quite happy when it was her turn to have her hair done. As she prepared to get up she said, "Now you sit here and look at this magazine."

As Ethel Barrett passed by she said, "My, you have an intelligent child with you!"

"With me?" said the gray-haired grandmother. "I never saw that kid before. I saw he needed discipline and decided to give it to him!"

For several years the experts have been telling parents that discipline would inhibit a child's development, and as the result of that advice many kids grew up without much guidance. We've reaped the effects today. But much of this has changed. Discipline has come back into style, at least in a measure.

> *Discipline—which is much different from punishment—enforces the teaching-learning process.*

What does discipline accomplish in the life of a youngster?

Here are five things which may well be an encouragement to you, whether you are a parent, a grandparent or a friend.

1. Discipline produces happy, well-adjusted children.

Ethel Barrett's story, which is true, illustrates that point. Hebrews 12:11 says, "No discipline seems pleasant at the time, but painful. Later on, however, it produces a harvest of righteousness and peace for those who have been trained by it." At the time discipline isn't pleasant—for those who give it and certainly for those who receive it. But the rewards produce maturity in life as well as in our relationship with God.

2. Discipline produces security for any child when he knows the boundaries of acceptable behavior.

No matter where you set limits, kids will push for just a bit more; however, when children understand how far they can go, there comes a security they can never have when parents won't say, "This is the limit!"

3. Discipline teaches obedience to parental authority.

Our English word discipline comes from the Latin word *discere,* which means "to know," and discipline gives the knowledge of right and wrong with the motivation to do right. Discipline—which is much different from punishment—enforces the teaching-learning process.

Insight

A study of successful men and women indicates that at some point in life they had to learn how to discipline themselves to be successful.

4. Discipline helps a child learn to assume responsibility.

Show me a man who is successful, and I'll show you someone who learned personal discipline somewhere, whether it was at home, in school or in the military. One of the traits of successful people is the ability to discipline themselves and subsequently accomplish a given task.

5. Discipline provides guidance and safety until a child is old enough to make reasoned value decisions on his own.

Discipline means everybody wins—parents and kids alike.

Think on This

If you have grown up in an environment without discipline, your first step is to begin taking small steps of discipline in your own life—promptness, keeping your word, maintaining order. Then do a study of what the Bible says about this whole area of our Christian experience—something neglected in the preaching and teaching of many churches. Once you are convinced, you will better assess the value of this in the lives of your children.

Resource Reading

Deuteronomy 11

ᴧᴧhen Parents Fail to Discipline

"He who spares the rod hates his son, but he who loves him is careful to discipline him." (Proverbs 13:24)

ᴧᴧhen an American teenager was found guilty of vandalizing an automobile in Singapore, he was sentenced to punishment by caning. Michael Fay, the teenager involved in the incident, generated a considerable amount of publicity all over the world. A great deal of public opinion came down on the side of the courts. "He got exactly what he deserved," said many. Some lawmakers were so impressed with the results that they introduced legislation enabling authorities to paddle wayward youths. This, they felt, would be an appropriate way of responding to growing juvenile crime and gang violence.

Others, of course, disagreed with the manner in which Singapore authorities dealt with juvenile crime and vandalism. In spite of the fact that the teenager broke the law, they felt that what the boy did didn't deserve the humiliation of having his backside thumped four times with a piece of cane. They contended that the punishment was too severe, too barbaric, too humiliating.

There is one thing for sure: In Singapore you will not find graffiti defacing buildings and highways. You won't find gum on the sidewalk or trash littering the highways. The government there runs a tight ship. Laws are rigidly enforced, and people know that " 'no' means 'no,' " and that if you ignore the law, there is a price to pay.

Please understand that the English-speaking people of Singapore do have an accent (to American ears), but for some reason kids there have still grown up understanding that the words *yes* and *no* mean exactly what they imply. In our desire to be loving, caring, understanding parents, we have grown soft on discipline and done our children a tremendous injustice by allowing them to get away with everything short of murder.

When we cannot discipline ourselves, life has a way of providing that discipline, and we suffer consequences of inestimable pain. Take, for example, the sad story of a young woman, a mother of a beautiful little girl now starting school, who will never live to see her daughter graduate from high school. Why? One time she couldn't say no to a friend, and she contracted AIDS. What a price to pay.

> *When we cannot discipline ourselves, life has a way of providing that discipline, and we suffer consequences of inestimable pain.*

I'm also thinking of a gifted and articulate career woman, happily married and wanting a baby of her own. But the sad reality is that she will never cradle her own child in her arms. Her husband of some twenty years brought into the marriage an infection which was eventually cured but left her unable to bear children. What a price to pay, what a terrible thing to inflict on someone you love because you can't discipline yourself and say no to a few moments of pleasure.

The Bible says, "Do not be deceived: God cannot be mocked. A man reaps what he sows. The one who sows to please his sinful nature, from that nature will reap destruction; the one who sows to please the Spirit, from the Spirit will reap eternal life" (Galatians 6:7-8). Paul's words are not harsh or opinionated. They simply describe the reality of nature and life itself.

When we parents fail to discipline ourselves and then our children, life ultimately does it for us and the consequences are cruel and much harsher than that which a Singapore court decrees. Think about it.

> ## Insight
>
> *Learning to discipline ourselves is much like having a burglar alarm in your home but not bothering to turn it on. When you least think that you need it, it may be the one time when you absolutely need it.*

Think on This

1. Sit down and take a few minutes to ponder what God is telling you personally.
2. Make a list of areas in your own personal life which need improvement. Now put the list in your wallet or purse and get it out every day this week and reflect on it.

3. Develop an action plan to help you break out of the indifference you have had.

Resource Reading
Galatians 6:1-10

God's Instruction, Teaching and Guidance

*"I will instruct you and teach you in the way you should go;
I will guide you with My eye." (Psalm 32:8, NKJV)*

Then an acquaintance told me about having to drive across 5,000 kilometers of snow and ice visiting outstations in the frozen wastelands of Siberia where there were roads, I asked, "How do you know where you are going?"

He replied, "Just a compass!"

"Have you ever heard of a GPS unit?" I inquired.

"A what?" he said.

"It's global positioning by satellite," I explained, telling him that the small handheld unit took a fix on some fourteen satellites and then pinpointed your location with precise accuracy. His eyes widened with excitement.

That day, I sent an e-mail to our Guidelines office. The staff found a GPS unit, sent it by overnight express to a friend who the next day flew some 7,000 miles and brought it with him. Within three days, the man who would have used his compass had a far more accurate means of knowing where he was as he started his journey across Siberia in winter.

Direction in our world is important, but in your personal life, it is even more important. Many explorers have died of thirst or hunger, knowing that water or food was nearby but unable to find it.

In Psalm 32, God gave a promise to David. Three verbs provide guidance when it comes to knowing where to go with your life. God said, "I will instruct you and teach you in the way you should go; I will guide you with My eye" (32:8, NKJV). How does He provide direction? First, He says, "I will instruct you." Second, "I will teach you." Third, "I will guide you with My eye."

> *As a loving Father, God instructs us, teaches us and guides us with His eye.*

Instruction and teaching are entirely different. You can read a book on computer science and be completely lost. Better to take a class in which a teacher gives instructions. Better still for someone to sit down with you and say, "Look, I'll show you how to do it. You start by turning on the computer. . . ." Having someone show you step-by-step is a lot easier and more meaningful than reading a book or even taking a class.

When God says, "I will guide you with My eye," does it means just what it says? Can you communicate with a simple look?

My son would suggest that you can! When he was a boy of about seven, one Sunday evening he positioned himself on the front row of the church where I was pastoring and proceeded to launch spit wads in a variety of directions. His mother, who was playing the piano, was no threat.

When I caught him glancing furtively at me, I narrowed my eyes, saying, "Stop it. Now!" (Strong nonverbal communication!)

Thinking that I would forget about it later, he ignored me. It was time for me to speak, so I stood and addressed the group saying, "Before our study tonight, we will have one more song." As the song leader grabbed a book and searched for something to sing, I went down from the platform, took my son by the hand and led him down the side aisle to the patio, where we had a heart-to-heart talk.

The singing was just finishing when the two of us came down the aisle. Steve was muffling

Insight

Just as we can give direction to a child simply by catching his eye in nonverbal communication, so God by His Spirit will give us guidance when we are sensitive to Him.

a few furtive sobs and I preached. People have long since forgotten what I spoke on, but those who were there will never forget what I did.

As a loving Father, God instructs us, teaches us and guides us with His eye. How can we miss His will and purpose for our lives? Yes, He still guides with His eye! May we understand clearly what He is saying lest we also face the consequences of disobedience.

Think on This

Is your relationship with your youngster close enough so that you can communicate simply by looking at him? Do you find that one child is more sensitive to you than another?

Resource Reading

Psalm 32

Talking to Your Kids about Sex

"So God created man in his own image, in the image of God he created him; male and female he created them." (Genesis 1:27)

Almost everybody is talking about sex these days—on TV, in the movies, on talk shows on radio and in casual conversation. Almost everybody, that is, except parents.

Take your youngster to the beach. Take him to the grocery store and in the checkout line your child looks over some of the rather lurid covers of the tabloids and magazines. There isn't much left to the imagination.

The problem is, however, that much of what a child sees is a far cry from reality and certainly from what God intended when it comes to the place of sex in our lives.

Why talk to your children about sex? Because your failure to deal with this important topic means that he may get a mixed-up or perverted picture of the whole situation. And that is what you don't want.

Why are we adults so hesitant to deal with this subject in a factual, straightforward manner, giving it the spin that God intends, helping our kids to understand why we must respect each other and be aware that our bodies are private? Perhaps the answer is that we grew up with hang-ups because our own parents were silent in seventeen languages and turned beet-red when we asked questions, leaving us with the distinct feeling that sex is something which ought not to be discussed, at least with adults.

The following guidelines will help you know how and when to talk to your kids about this important topic.

> *Sex education is too personal, too important to be left to school or church. It's a parent's responsibility.*

Realize your failure to deal with the subject will result in his getting sex education from another source.

The source could be another child, a pornographic maga-zine, a web site or a distorted and perhaps perverted source. It's part of life and should neither be avoided or considered something that creates embarrassment. My conviction is that sex education is too personal, too important to be left to school or church. It's a parent's responsibility. Period!

You need to get the facts straight yourself.

I am amazed at the ignorance of many adults when it comes to the function of the human body and how a baby is grown. Procreation is one of the absolutely amazing phenomena of existence. When you talk to a little child, avoid vulgar or slang terms. Children can understand proper terms and accept them as readily as synonyms.

Answer questions as they arise.

A rule of thumb is to tell a child what he wants to know. Give him an answer that satisfies, and do it when the question is asked.

Put into practice in your home the values that you feel are important.

In a real sense you are the sex-education program your youngster needs, which includes hugs, good-night kisses and embracing, the reality that Mom and Dad love each other and that we respect each other's privacy. If you have a good marriage, your kids will see that. But your children and teens need to understand that sex is not for kids but for married adults. By teaching your child that sex is a beautiful, meaningful relationship for a husband and a wife, you are helping a youngster understand a value which has been neglected and badly distorted.

> ### Insight
>
> *Your child is going to get sex education. The only question is from what source? Other children, perhaps some of the sources mentioned here, or from you—it's your call.*

Make sure your child understands that his body is private.

As much as we wish it were not necessary, we can't ignore the danger that confronts kids growing up today: all strangers cannot be trusted. An attitude or suspicion or distrust of everyone isn't necessary, but keeping the kind of a relationship with your youngster that makes it easy for him to talk to you is important.

Think about it, and then talk about it. It's all part of your job as a parent.

Think on This

Answer questions as they come up, giving enough information to satisfy, using straightforward language, answering questions in a straightforward, matter-of-fact manner.

Resource Reading

Genesis 1

Sex Is Not for Kids

"They made me the keeper of the vineyards; but mine own vineyard have I not kept." (Song of Solomon 1:6, KJV)

We're living in a global village, and whether or not you like it, life has become much the same for people in Manila, Los Angeles, Bucharest and Sydney. You can eat at the same franchises, wear the same brand clothes and watch the same TV programs—which produces a staleness and predictable behavior.

I thought of that recently when, in a period of a week, two rather shocking articles came across my desk, both dealing with teens, both pointing out that kids between the ages of ten and fourteen are far more sexually active than their parents or teachers have any inkling of. One article—a *Time* magazine feature—was entitled, "Where'd You Learn That?" and described American teens.[15] The other article came from the *Manila Bulletin*, some 8,000 miles removed from the U.S., and was captioned, "Filipino 10 to 14-year-olds engaging in sex? You'd be surprised!"

Both articles cited three factors in the tremendous acceleration of sexual activity among kids hardly old enough to shave or wear perfume: the access to the media and the sexual exposure which it brings, absentee parents or working parents who are uninvolved in the lives of their teens, and social pressures from their peers.

"Three powerful forces have shaped today's child prodigies," says *Time* magazine, "a prosperous information age that increasingly promotes products and entertains audiences by titillation; aggressive public-policy initiates that loudly preach sexual responsibility, further desensitizing kids to the subject; and the decline of two-parent households, which leaves adolescents with little supervision."[16]

My response is not knee-jerk but conditioned by reality. I have to ask two sobering questions: 1. Where have the parents gone? 2. Why is the church so silent and ineffective in making a difference in our culture and environment?

Parents who are not there when a youngster comes home from school by default allow the media to become the major influence in their child's life. Dragging your youngster to church on Sunday or casually asking, "How did your day go?" doesn't counter the impact of five hours of television a day or the power of a peer group.

You are a parent, and there is nothing under God's heaven which substitutes for your presence.

There is no substitute for being there, for knowing who is on the telephone and what the lyrics are to the music that your teens listen to, knowing whether your kid is doing homework or watching MTV. You are a parent, and there is nothing under God's heaven which substitutes for your presence.

Why can't the church be more than a voice of conscience crying, "Naughty! Naughty! Don't do that!"? In a list of items asking church kids to rate where they needed spiritual help, the vast majority of youth who were interviewed said, "The church tells me what *not* to do but doesn't tell me *what* to do." They have a point.

Sexuality is very much a part of life and the Bible has a lot to say about its place in our lives. God didn't give us the advice in Scripture to take away the fun or excitement but to give us guidance and happiness.

When the Bible decries premarital sex it is with reason that goes far beyond what we think of as Victorian prudishness. Apart from marriage, sexual relations will never meet the deep emotional needs of either partner. But the emotional scarring and damage of causal sex can take a lifetime to heal.

> ## Insight
>
> *Our neglecting to talk openly and specifically about sex sends a message of indifference. Talking about it lets teens know that we care and accept responsibility for what they do. It also gives us the opportunity of talking about how God views this part of our lives.*

Regardless of what happens in our culture and society, there is good news: God's purpose in our lives continues to be beneficent and purposeful. It's still the good news in a bad-news world.

Think on This

1. How many afternoons last week was your teen at home alone?

2. Have you talked about STDs, AIDS and pregnancy with your teen?
3. Is it possible that your teenager may be sexually active and you prefer not to know about it?

Resource Reading

Ephesians 6:1-4

Laying the Foundation of Faith

*"These commandments that I give you today are to
be upon your hearts. Impress them on your children.
Talk about them when you sit at home and when
you walk along the road, when you lie down and
when you get up." (Deuteronomy 6:6-7)*

If you as a parent are depending on an hour's visit to a local church to offset the influence of a secular world in
the life of your child, forget it! You are up against tougher
competition than you can handle. Altogether too often we
commute to a church not too far away from home where we
can spend an hour in air-conditioned comfort while our children are in Sunday school or "junior church." Kids color pictures, sing some songs, watch a video and have crackers and
Kool-aid before they hear a frustrated teacher tell a Bible story
which often sounds like something akin to a fairy tale.

A mother discovered this when she questioned her child
about the Bible lesson of the morning. The child embellished
the story a little, so the mother asked, "Are you *sure* that's the
way it was?"

"Well," said the youngster, "you'd never believe it the way
the teacher told it."

The real problem isn't the quality of Christian education—it is the amount of it, and the odds which are against it. If your youngster spends thirty-five hours in public school, then, along with the 3 R's, he will get sex education, evolution and social theories which run counter to much of what he learns at church. In addition, there's the impact of the great educator which is prominently displayed in your family or living room, otherwise know as a television set—or should we call it the video worship center?

The latest figures are that the average TV glows in vivid, living color five and a half hours a day. By the time your youngster graduates from high school, he will have seen 15,000 to 20,000 hours of television and will have witnessed 25,000 acts of violence including rapes, murders and aggression.

hy not set aside some time each day, even if it is as brief as five minutes following a meal, when you as a family touch God together?

But won't kids just "pick up" Christian values by growing up in a Christian home? Sure, just like they pick up science and math and become excellent musicians by just growing up in a home where parents have those abilities. It is true that some things are "caught" not "taught," but when it comes to offsetting the secular influence that surrounds our children, we need a frontal attack.

You feed your kids daily, right? You expect them to study their lessons daily. You want them to practice daily to learn proficiency in music. Why not set aside some time each day, even if it is as brief as five minutes following a meal, when you as a family touch God together? This prayer time can be tremendously meaningful in the lives of your children.

After God gave the Ten Commandments at Mt. Sinai, Moses commanded the people to walk in the ways of the Lord and to teach these commandments to their children. He said:

These commandments that I give you today are to be upon your hearts. Impress them on your children. Talk about them when you sit at home and when you walk along the road, when you lie down and when you get up. (Deuteronomy 6:6-7)

He put the responsibility of morality and integrity on the shoulders of parents, who, in turn, convey spiritual truths to their children.

Most people call this time "Family Devotions" or "Family Worship." No matter what you call it, it's important. Several ingredients should go into the mix: 1. Scripture itself, including memorizing portions of the great book which stay with your children forever; 2. learning to pray for each

Insight

With our busy lives it becomes very easy to assume that our kids will get the core experience of our faith by just being in a Christian home and by being in church-related activities. Don't assume anything. Taking time to plant the Word in the heart of a child will be amply rewarded by seeing it come to fruition in the teenager or young adult he becomes.

other's needs and the needs of the world; and 3. learning to care about each other as families should.

There are some things which need to be done in time . . . for eternity!

Think on This

For family devotions,

1. Use a modern translation of Scripture.
2. Involve all the members of the family.
3. Never allow older children to make fun of what younger children say or pray about.
4. Use variety.
5. Make sure you use the mix of the three ingredients suggested.
6. Reward children when they have excelled in memorization and application. (Note: Incentives are a means of affirming excellence, not bribery to do what a child really doesn't want to do.)

Resource Reading
Deuteronomy 6:1-7

A Culture of Violence

"The LORD examines the righteous, but the wicked and those who love violence his soul hates." (Psalm 11:5)

"Dear Dr. Sala, should I let my three-year-old boy play with toy guns?" asks a mother who listens to Guidelines. She says, "Even if I don't buy him toy guns, he takes his finger and points it and says 'Boom, boom!' " In a culture of violence, how does a mother concerned about the values she is teaching her child put an asbestos barrier between violence and her child?

No generation of children has ever been raised in a culture that has so tolerated and condoned violence. Television, movies, computer games, the Internet and the examples of adults have wiped out the line of demarcation between reality and fantasy, between right and wrong. Working or absentee parents who are disinterested or too busy to make a difference in the lives of their children have defaulted on the responsibility of teaching the difference between straight lines and crooked ones.

Responding to the question of why there is so much youthful violence today—an issue forced upon us after the massacre at Columbine High School in Littleton, Colorado—the following response from an eighteen-year-old teenager by the name of Sarah Roney was widely circulated on the Internet:

We live in a loosely tied society, a culture dedicated to death. If you don't want the kid, kill it. If you don't want to live out the rest of your God-given days, kill yourself. Or better yet, have someone else come help you do it. I guess no matter how horrible or gruesome or gut-wrenching it may be, it was just a matter of time before someone got that "killing-as-a-means-to-an-end" idea stuck in their head for the part between birth and death as well. Everything that happens in a family and cities and states and countries is the mirror image of the big picture.

This young woman faults parents for the attitudes and dismal conduct of her generation, parents who are not there for their kids, parents who (in her words), never say, " 'If you don't shape up by the time I count to three . . .' *and then really count to three.*" She adds sadly, "We are running wild and pretty soon we're going to be too far from home to ever get back."

Violence among youth today is not simply an American problem. It's a universal issue because the teens of Europe along with the Philippines and Latin America, and—yes, even China to a large degree—are watching the same movies, listening to the same music and being influenced by the same people.

> *No generation of children has ever been raised in a culture that has so tolerated and condoned violence.*

No, not all teenagers have surrounded themselves with the culture of death and violence. Those who have are in a small but growing minority, yet the vast percentage of teens today are good kids who do their homework, take care of brothers and sisters, attend church and Bible study and are involved in building, not destroying, the world in which they live.

Yet—and this is where I turn the corner—I am not content to lose any of the next generation. Every casualty is someone's son or daughter, a person of value and worth in the sight of God. Jesus said, "For the Son of Man has come to seek and to save that which was lost" (Luke 19:10, NKJV).

If you are a parent, the

Insight

*O*ur sensibilities were shocked when a six-year-old boy found a loaded gun, took it to school and pulled the trigger in a classroom, taking the life of a classmate. While the little boy's future life will be forever smirched, the little girl was deprived of ever having a future.

gift of yourself—your time, your interest in your teen's world, your leading the way spiritually—is the most valuable gift you can give. There is no substitute for yourself.

Think on This

1. Do you have firearms in your home? Do they have trigger locks? Are they locked? Are the ammo and the firearm separated?
2. While it is highly unlikely that you can completely keep your children from playing with toy guns (whether they are squirt guns or cap guns), you can minimize violence by

not buying toys, computer CDs or video games that include violence.

3. Find out what wholesome, educational videos and games
which are also entertaining and positive are available.
(Yes, there are plenty of them on the market. Take the
time to check them out.)

4. Don't hesitate to return to the store any game, toy or video
that includes violence.

Resource Reading

Ephesians 6

You Can Always Tell a Teenager (But You Can't Always Tell 'Em Very Much)

"Train a child in the way he should go, and when he is old he will not turn from it." (Proverbs 22:6)

ack in the days when computers booted under DOS, I put a line in my autoexec.bat which put a message on the screen reading, "Remember, this too shall pass!" That's also the way it is with those years called teen years. When you've got a teenager in the house, you sometimes wonder, *Will we survive until he is on his own?* You've got to remember, "This too shall pass!"

For many today the emotional passage from childhood to adulthood is like surviving a tornado or a hurricane. It's a battle. Kids don't like it any better than parents do, but it's a very important period of a youngster's life. Psychologist Dr. Henry Brandt says, "Your children will need your guidance the most between ages sixteen and twenty," yet often those years are the most difficult in terms of a parent's telling a teenager what to do.

Why? Kids know it all! It's we parents who are not very bright. Mark Twain once said, at age sixteen, his dad was about the dumbest person in the world, but he was amazed how much the old man had learned by the time he turned twenty-one. There's a scientific reason for this entire problem: at age sixteen a kid's brain goes out his ear for a drink of water and doesn't return until about age twenty-one. On second thought, that may not be scientific, but sometimes it does happen.

> **N**eeded: *more models, fewer critics; more prayer, less preaching.*

Lest I leave the wrong impression, especially with my teenage friends, I must say that all generalizations are not valid. All teenagers are not struggling with drugs, alcohol or their sexuality. To the contrary, thousands and thousands of young men and women are working hard, studying, talking to adults (even parents), attending church and involved in community affairs, preparing to take their places in the world of the twenty-first century. A growing multitude of teenagers are committed to Jesus Christ and to biblical principles, including sexual abstinence. But they are the ones you *don't* hear about. (Ever see a sign which reads, "Nice dog! Does not bite!"?)

Sadly enough, it is usually the exception which draws the printer's ink and the feature in the evening news. On high school and college campuses today a quiet multitude of student groups meet under the sponsorship of Inter-Varsity, Campus Crusade, Athletes in Action and local Bible study groups. They are providing answers to the questions of youth, helping them traverse the troubled waters of adolescence.

I am convinced that when we see a teenager who has failed, we are often looking at the product of parental failure. A child learns half of everything he knows by age three and three-fourths by age seven. In far too many cases, during those important years a youngster is deprived of instruction and care and left to grow up with a television set for a tutor and a baby-sitter for a surrogate mother.

In some cases you can't help the fact that you have to work, but you can still fight back by being the person God would have you to be by: 1. taking your youngster to church—and staying, 2. by turning off the television set and reading to your child, 3. by teaching right from wrong and 4. striving to be the person you really want your child to become.

Too often it is not until we are confronted with disaster as a teenager hits the wall that we get serious about what's happening to our teens.

> ## Insight
>
> *Keeping the lines of communication open with your teenager is one of the most positive things you can do to combat the conflict between parents and their teens.*

Then we parents put blame on our children's friends, teachers and the culture that surrounds us—when the real problem is parental failure. Needed: more models, fewer critics; more prayer, less preaching; fewer who tell kids what to do and more who do it. May God help us! And yes, He will.

Think on This

1. When you sense that a teenager in your house wants to talk, you had better listen, or the time may come when you would give almost anything to know what's going on in his head.
2. How much unstructured time do you spend with your teens?
3. What do you do for just plain fun?
4. Asking, "What do you think about . . . ?" helps open topics for discussion.

Resource Reading

Proverbs 19:1-18

Understanding Teenagers

> "The king was shaken. He went up to the room
> over the gateway and wept. As he went, he said:
> 'O my son Absalom! My son, my son Absalom!
> If only I had died instead of you—O Absalom,
> my son, my son!' " (2 Samuel 18:33)

Those teenage years are often a difficult season of life,
few would deny—either parents or teenagers themselves. For some, those teenage years are more like a battle to
be fought than a transition to be experienced, but for others,
those years are a very good time when a teenager grows to maturity, becoming the young adult that a parent hoped he
would be.

Youth has been described as a transition from the organization of childhood to the disorganization of youth, resulting in
the reorganization of adulthood. A frustrated parent said
there is but one thing to do when a youngster turns thirteen:
take him out in the backyard and bury him in a barrel with the
plug left out of the barrel. Then when he turns sixteen, drive
in the plug.

Mark Twain was right when he said, "Life would be infinitely happier if we could only be born at the age of eighty and
gradually approach eighteen." But no one chooses at what age
he is born. Neither do you choose your parents. On either side

of the issue, for good or bad, you're stuck with what you've got.

Being the parent of a teenager requires the balance of a tightrope walker and the skill of a diamond cutter. Both balance and skill are necessary. One of the reasons that it's tough being the parent of a teenager is that the goals of a parent and a teenager are usually at cross-purposes.

What is the goal of a teenager? Independence. And what is the goal of a parent? Maturity. Independence to a teenager is "freedom to do anything I want!" which can result in irresponsibility. But maturity to a parent is making right decisions, which results in responsibility.

> *Support is necessary, but only until a teenager is able to withstand the winds and pressures of life today.*

Recently I planted a carrotwood tree in my front yard—a gangly little tree with three branches. Since the tree isn't strong enough to withstand a strong wind or certainly a climbing child, I had to put supporting stakes by the three branches. They are temporary, however. As soon as the tree is strong enough to support itself, those stakes have to come down. And the sooner the better! So is it with our children. Support is necessary, but only until a teenager is able to withstand the winds and pressures of life today—something which a great many teenagers are not doing very well.

The psalmist likens children to arrows in the hands of an archer (see Psalm 127:4-5). Anyone who ever held a bow in his hand and notched an arrow quickly learns that how firmly you

hold the bow and how you release the arrow has everything to
do with hitting the target.

Pull the bowstring back too far or hold onto it too long
and you will overdrive the target. But pull it back only a little way and release it too soon and your arrow will fall
short of the target. So is it with a teenager. Hold on to them
too long and you have re-
bellion and anger, but release them too soon and
they fall short of the target and get into trouble.

Unfortunately, there is
no scale anywhere in the
world that says your teenager is ready to handle life
at age sixteen or seven-
teen or at five-foot-seven
or at six-three. Every
teenager is different.
Some are quite mature at
fourteen, and others at
age nineteen still play
with their toy boats in the
bath.

> ### Insight
>
> *One of the major rea-
> sons that the teen years
> are difficult is that the
> goals of parents and their
> teens are at cross-
> purposes; however, when
> you understand this, you
> at least have a framework
> for conflict resolution.*

The psalmist wrote,
"Sons are a heritage from the LORD, children a reward from
him" (Psalm 127:3). It's true—even of teenagers!

Think on This

1. While some things are nonnegotiable (morality, respect
   for parents, honesty, etc.), there are some issues which

can be mutually negotiated. What are some of those in your household?

2. When parents do not stand together, what kind of a message does this send to your teen?

3. When you suspect that your mate said no to something your teen wants to do, ask, "Did you talk with your mom/dad about this? What did he/she say? Well, that's what I say as well." Remember, you hang together or you hang separately.

Resource Reading

2 Samuel 18

Ten Commandments for Parents of Teens

"Fathers, do not embitter your children, or they will become discouraged. . . . Whatever you do, work at it with all your heart, as working for the Lord." (Colossians 3:21, 23)

One of the reasons it's difficult being a teenager is that emotional maturity rarely matches physical maturity. It's tough being a teenager, probably more so today than ever before, but it's not impossible. A parent is a coach, a teacher, a chaplain, a mentor, a model and, hopefully, a friend as well. Teen years can be a blessing or a battle, and the parents—not the teenager—usually decide which it will be.

What can parents do to make the transition from childhood to adulthood a blessing instead of a battle? Plenty! I'm calling that answer "Ten Commandments for Parents of Teens!"

Commandment #1: Thou shalt remember that the teen years are a transitional time.

A teenager is in the process of becoming. Those years are marked by three things: 1. ambivalence (both a child and an adult are battling for the same body); 2. growth; and 3. peer pressure—more so today than ever before.

Commandment #2: Thou shalt be a *parent*.

Parenting is the raising of children by parents, not the raising of parents by children! You are in charge!

Commandment #3: Thou shalt keep the channels of communication open.

A person becomes a teenager just one day at a time. Communication doesn't die at age thirteen. If it ceases, it is usually, though not always, because the parents haven't been there to listen. Scores of teens and parents communicate openly and freely and bring each other into their respective worlds.

Commandment #4: Thou shalt sift the trivial from the important.

Parents need to ask, "Will this scar, or does it just annoy me?" If you saw a four-year-old playing with a knife, you'd do something and fast. Drugs, alcohol and promiscuous sex will scar too—for life.

> *Teen years can be a blessing or a battle, and the parents—not the teenager—usually decide which it will be.*

Commandment #5: Thou shalt use sarcasm and criticism sparingly.

Teens come up with statements that are real shockers, and they do it in a matter-of-fact sort of way. Strive to help your teenager see cause and effect—like what happens when a fourteen-year-old girl chooses to try to raise a baby.

Commandment #6: Don't impose your own unfulfilled ambitions on your teenager.

Discover what your teen's unique gifts are and guide him accordingly. That's part of what the advice of Proverbs 22:6 is about: "Train a child in the way he should go, and when he is old he will not turn from it." Your child would never make it to med school but he's a computer whiz. Go with the flow of the natural aptitudes and abilities which God gave him.

Commandment #7: Thou shalt differentiate between acceptance and approval.

Sooner or later, almost every parent has to convey this message: "Look, I love you but I don't like what you are doing. I think it is wrong!" But don't throw the baby out with the bath.

> <u>Insight</u>
>
> *Generally you get from the teen years what you expect: they can be an ongoing battle or a wonderful time of self-realization.*

Commandment #8: Thou shalt give your child an undivided portion of unconditional love.

Never base love on performance.

Commandment #9: Thou shalt give of your time as well as your money.

It's a tragedy to give a child money, education and culture but to withhold the most important gift of all—that of yourself.

Commandment #10: Thou shalt surround your child with a fence of prayer.

The time may come when a teenager may ignore your advice and spurn your wisdom, but he cannot escape your prayers.

Think on This

1. Realize that teens communicate on their time frame—not yours—which means that if you don't listen to them when they want to talk, the time may come when you would give anything to have a meaningful conversation but it won't happen.
2. A youngster becomes a teen one day at a time, which means that if communication is poor between a parent and a teen, it has been that way for a long time but just unrecognized.
3. Lay the groundwork for communication by unstructured time (when you have no agenda) together.

Resource Reading
Ephesians 5:15-6:4

Is Anyone Listening?

*"Do not be amazed at this, for a time is coming when
all who are in their graves will hear his voice and come
out—those who have done good will rise to live,
and those who have done evil will rise to be
condemned." (John 5:28-29)*

Looking back, the mother said that the problems started
with her nineteen-year-old son when he was turned
down at the school he wanted to attend. About then he
started drinking pretty heavily and started smoking pot.
"Makes me feel better," he said. His appearance took a hit too.
He had been pretty clean and well groomed, but now his hair
grew long and dirty. He stopped bathing regularly and seemed
to be withdrawn and sullen. He often shut himself in his room
and listened to rock music. "I wish I were dead," he told a
friend.

When his mother would ask him to come on out of his
room and be sociable, he would yell, "Leave me alone—I'm all
right!" He gave away his prized collection of CDs and cas-
settes—the music that he listened to hour after hour.

Then it happened. Suddenly and unexplainably, according
to his mother, he ended his life with an overdose of drugs that
could not have been an accident. A terse suicide note said,
"I'm sorry for having messed up my life, but there is no way
out."

When tragedy struck, people said, "How could he do that? He had everything to live for. Something must have snapped!" But the fact was his death was neither sudden nor without warning.

Almost everything I have described was a warning, a red flag which no one seemed to notice. Are there signs friends and parents should see that should tell us something is wrong, something very serious? Yes, but too often we see them only in retrospect.

> *Never, under any circumstances, should even the casual threat of suicide be taken lightly.*

What are some of those indications that things are not right?

1. Isolation and loneliness
2. Contacts with other people—especially authority figures, close friends and family—become shallow and without real meaning
3. A preoccupation with death
4. Changes in both sleep patterns and appetites; and those changes go both ways—from habitual sleep to insomnia, from eating practically nothing to eating so much there are rapid weight gains
5. A loss of interest in what has previously been meaning-ful—school, music, sports or work
6. A breakdown in communication as an individual becomes withdrawn and introspective
7. An uncharacteristic burst of generosity—even the tidying up of a room that has previously looked like a disaster zone

8. Comments about suicide which may be a far more frank assessment of a situation than anyone realizes at the time
9. Depression and lethargy

Never, under any circumstances, should even the casual threat of suicide be taken lightly. People usually talk about what they eventually do.

What does a person do when some of these signs are present? The head of a suicide prevention hotline suggests three things: *listen, listen, listen.* He believes that most suicides are a desperate cry for someone to be heard.

Skip the advice. Don't waste your breath saying, "Snap out of it—everything is going to be OK." Save the sermons on how much you have to live for, but listen and take seriously the cry of a person whose problem may not seem very big to you but is life-threatening to the one who is depressed.

If what I have described is a picture of someone you know, get help for that person. It is far better to confront than to wish forever you had insisted on getting help. For some youth today, life doesn't appear to be terribly hopeful, yet to know that someone cares and will lis-

> ## Insight
>
> *When a youth takes his life, people often say, "How could this have happened? There was nothing that made us aware of his problem." The fact is, however, that he had been giving signals for some time but no one picked up on them.*

ten helps destroy despair and brings hope. Where there is life, there is yet hope.

Think on This

1. If someone you know ever threatens to take his life, then says, "I didn't mean it!" you must not take that lightly. Remember, people usually talk about what they do.

2. Resist the desire to moralize or pass judgment on what your teen may say before you give the whole situation a full hearing. Then approach a situation with which you disagree, saying, "How do you think God views this situation? What do you think about our taking some time to dig out Scripture and both of us find out?"

Resource Reading

John 10

Teen Suicides

*"For to me, to live is Christ
and to die is gain." (Philippians 1:21)*

The number of teen suicides has reached epidemic proportions today, and what is happening is not an isolated phenomenon in the United States but a disaster of worldwide proportions. Suicide is taking the lives of some of our finest, most talented young men and women. In the U.S., suicide is the second leading cause of death for teens, and overall the number of youthful suicides has increased by 300 percent in the last thirty years. For every youth who does take his life, there are thirty to fifty attempts, and behind every encounter or flirtation with death is a said statement: "Life has lost its purpose and meaning and I've given up on the hope that it can ever be different."[17]

In Japan the youth suicide rate has so alarmed civic officials that national programs of education have been established to stop the tragic loss of life. The same problems are confronting youth all over the world. Understanding the reasons why young men and women take their lives may help to prevent this ever happening to your family.

As the result of counseling and working with numerous families who have experienced youth suicides, I can isolate four factors that, I believe, contribute to the desperation of youth—resulting in suicide—today.

1. Inexperience

As an older adult you have faced challenges and some pretty tough situations before, and somehow, with God's help, you have made it—you got through. As a result, when you face problems that seem insurmountable, you do not quit or give up. You hang on and trust God. But kids have not been through as much trouble and hard times as you have. When they are confronted with loss or tragedy or depression, they feel that there is no way out and often despair of life itself.

2. The inability of youths to live up to their parents' expectations

This is especially true in Japan, where the failure to pass high school or college entrance exams means the end of the education road. Often when the kids fail, they feel they have disgraced their families and the insult is too great for them to bear. When parents have set up goals that are too high for a youth, or even the youth sets up for himself goals too high to attain, you have a problem. The inability to cope with that problem is one of the factors which has caused the suicide rate to jump drastically. The next two factors are related, almost two sides of the same coin.

3. Pessimism in our world which kids can't handle

The words of the songs sung by many of today's rock or heavy metal groups focus on dark themes—drugs, death and despair. Listening to those negative messages hour after hour, day after day becomes a burden kids can't bear. Without realizing that there is another side to the dark world, they often lose hope and give up on life.

4. A lack of faith which offsets despair and despondency

Sharrel Keyes was a suicide candidate. She tells about her experience in *His* magazine.
She says,

> The summer I started graduate school all of the superficiality and meaninglessness converged and pushed me into a crisis. I had to find some answers. Since I had just graduated with a minor in philosophy and religion, I turned back to my texts for answers. I read the existentialists, who said there is no meaning except in the present. There is no ultimate why. . . . There is nothing, simply nothing. I finally saw that the logical conclusion to their position was suicide. If there is no reason to be here, then there is no reason to be here now.[18]

Insight

One of the reasons for the pessimism and fatalism in the lives of some teens today is that they have not lived long enough to encounter difficult situations and see God bring them through. Lacking the experience an adult may have, they feel despair and hopelessness.

Fortunately two things happened to Sharrel that saved her life. The first was that she discovered C.S. Lewis and found a God who is holding everything together in a plan far bigger than she could see; and then she saw the irrationality of taking her own life through the suicidal death of a close friend.

Despair is reversed by even the slightest faith in God that looks beyond the circumstances to His ability and willingness to change things. Faith is believing promises about the future with few visible guarantees in the present, but it is this that gives you the assurance that life is meaningful. God lives and will honor the promises of His Word.

Think on This

Strive to help your kids know that no matter how difficult or hopeless a situation, no matter how desperate, how far from God he may think he is, there is hope because there is God. That truth can take any person through his darkest hour.

Resource Reading

1 Samuel 28

You Can't Always Fix It

"As for me, far be it from me that I should sin against the
LORD by failing to pray for you." (1 Samuel 12:23)

"Dear Dr. Sala," writes the parent of a college fresh-
man, "our son received D's and F's on his report
card and will not be allowed to go back to college this fall. Fur-
thermore, he won't listen to our counsel or advice. What
should we do?" The letter which I've just shared is a compos-
ite of more than a few which have come to us in recent
months. How far should a parent go? How much should a parent do? What does a parent really *owe* his youngster who is no
longer a child but acts like one?

I'm convinced that the most challenging and often frus-
trating years of parenting, at least for some, are not when
your kids are small, when you say, "Pick up your toys!" and
your youngster responds with minimal persuasion. They
are the years between the ages of sixteen and twenty-four,
when a young person is convinced that he is fully mature,
and a parent recognizes he is physically mature enough to
be dangerous but not emotionally mature enough to handle some situations.

When do you give advice? When do you bite your tongue
and keep your mouth shut? When do you dip into your
meager savings to finance higher education and when do

you say, "It's time for you to go to work and support yourself!" Ready for some simple, clear-cut answers?

I'm sorry to disappoint you, but I don't have any. Simplistic answers don't fit every situation! Here's why. Kids mature at different rates. One youngster is very mature at age fifteen; another is still a ten-year-old in a nineteen-year-old's body. One kid knows exactly what he wants to do with his life and does it. Another changes his major in college six times before settling down. One youngster makes his bed at midnight when he gets up for a snack. Another, with the same parents, has a room which is an absolute disaster zone, off-limits to all but the very brave.

A wise parent strives to help a youngster understand he is responsible for his own life. You love your kids, you feed them, you guide them, but ultimately they are responsible for their own choices. Maybe it would be better for a youngster to drop out of college for a year or two to gain practical work experience in the real world, and then decide what he wants to do with his life.

> *A wise parent strives to help a youngster understand he is responsible for his own life.*

Dad, Mom, there may come a time when your kids reject your counsel and advice. They may spurn your wisdom, but they cannot escape your prayers.

Don't expect trouble or your expectations may become self-fulfilling prophecies. I have to admit that the young adulthood years for my three were a most fulfilling time of parenting, a whole lot more fun for us than diapers and dishwater hands. But I can tell you one thing for sure, when your teenager makes the decision to do right and to walk with the Lord because it is what he wants to do—not what you want done—you'll sleep better at night.

Think on This

1. Have you taken prayer seriously? To find out more about prayer, work through my book *Touching God: 52 Guidelines for Personal Prayer* available through a local Christian bookstore or this publisher.

Insight

At some point you have to say about your young adult, "Lord, there's nothing else I can do. Will You please take over and do what I cannot do?" and leave the situation in His hands.

2. The Bible tells us to pray about everything, and everything means exactly that—your teenager and his world and problems, knowing when to talk about issues, when to confront, when to say, "I love you too much to let you do this" or to pray, simply awaiting God's timing about a situation.

Resource Reading

Genesis 49

And Your Children after You

*"But as for me and my household,
we will serve the LORD." (Joshua 24:15)*

"Dear Dr. Sala," wrote a gray-haired father well into his seventies, "one of my greatest heartaches is that my children are not living for the Lord. They were all raised in a Christian home. In fact, my wife and I have spent most of our lives in the Lord's service, but more than anything else, we would like to see them come back to Him before we die."

Nothing can be more distressing than feeling strongly about certain values, including our relationship with God, and then seeing our children reject those values and turn their backs on God. Scores of letters have come to me from you who have unburdened your heart, laden with guilt, because you are convinced that you did something wrong. In many cases, it is that your child has a mind of his own and has chosen to walk a path that causes you to lie awake nights worrying over him.

Can we as Christian parents hold on to the expectation that God will honor His Word and, in time, turn the hearts of our children toward heaven? Are there definite promises which we can hold, asking God in faith to honor His Word?

Be very sure that God will honor what He has promised in His Word no matter what the time frame may be, whether you live to see it or it comes together long after your influence has paled in death.

Are there substantial promises in Scripture which extend to our children? The answer is, "Yes!"

On the Day of Pentecost Peter promised that the gift of the Holy Spirit was "for you and your children and for all who are far off—for all whom the Lord our God will call" (Acts 2:39). When the jailer at Philippi was concerned about his own safety (jailers who had prisoners escape under their watch could lose their loves in recompense for what happened), Paul and Silas said, "Believe in the Lord Jesus, and you will be saved—you and your household" (16:31). The Roman household included not only children but servants as well.

> *God will honor what He has promised in His Word whether you live to see it or it comes together long after your influence has paled in death.*

These promises, of course, don't deny the child the power of choice or eliminate the stubborn will of a youngster who wants a taste of the world. Nor does it suggest that your children do not have to make the same transactions of faith that you had to make, but it does give you as a parent confidence to trust God in the meanwhile.

If you need further encouragement, let me share one more thought with you. In the Old Testament, there are two passages which ask the question, "Is there anything too hard for the Lord?" and both of those passages are followed by promises that extend to our children. Is that merely a coincidence, or is God saying specifically that nothing is too hard for Him, including changing the stubborn will of a prodigal son or daughter and pointing that one back toward home and heaven? Those two promises are Genesis 18:14 and Jeremiah 32:27.

Long ago, when Judah and his brothers went down to Egypt and the youngest, Benjamin, was detained, the oldest brother, who bore responsibility for the lad, asked, "How shall I go up to my father, and the lad be not with me?" (Genesis 44:34, KJV). That's a question every parent must ask in relationship to our Heavenly Father, "How shall I go up to my Father, at the end of life, and my children not be with me?" Think about it.

Insight

When you pray for your children to follow the Lord, you can be sure that you are praying for God's will (see 1 Timothy 2:4; 2 Peter 3:9, Acts 2:39 and Acts 16:31), so you can pray in faith, trusting Him.

Think on This

1. If you believe God will honor His Word regarding your family, don't say, "My son is not a Christian." Rather in faith say, "My son hasn't yet trusted the Lord but I am confident that He will."

2. If you came to Christ after your children were grown, after much prayer, sit down with them. Let them know that you didn't know the Lord when they were growing up, which accounted for your failure to introduce them to spiritual

things. Explain that now that you have now come to understand this, you very much would like to see them find out for themselves.

Resource Reading

Joshua 24:14-27

A Final Word

Regis Philbin of the TV show "Who Wants to Be a Millionaire?" made famous the question, "Is that your final answer?" For us who are parents, only God has the final answer! But the good news is that He *does* have the answer, and when we get to the end of ourselves and there still seem to be no answers, we can quietly say, "God, we need Your help! We aren't sure what to do!"

A famous Old Testament dad whose son attempted to wrest the kingdom from him cried out, "When my heart is overwhelmed: lead me to the rock that is higher than I" (Psalm 61:2, KJV). God met David, and He will meet you as well.

Raising kids is much like swimming horses across a river. When you are out there in the current, you wonder if you are ever going to get across.

But you will! And God will be with you each step of the way!

Yes, we have no alternative but to confront our culture if we are going to protect our kids from what can sweep them downstream to Sodom. Someday you will look back and reminisce. You will not trade the tears, the joys and the experiences of watching your child grow to maturity for anything in the world. It is one of the truly great experiences of life. May God make those years as precious and meaningful to you as they have been for Darlene and me. Keep your Bible and the Band-Aids handy! They are both necessary. And enjoy the parenting journey.

If we can provide further help, contact us. You can write to me or send e-mail to the following:

In the United States:

Dr. Harold J. Sala
Guidelines International Ministries
Box G
Laguna Hills, CA 92654
www.guidelines.org
E-mail: guidelines@guidelines.org

In Asia:

Dr. Harold J. Sala
Guidelines International Ministries
Box 4000
Makati, MM
Philippines

Endnotes

1. Glenn Doman, personal correspondence with the author, September 20, 2000.

2. "How Could This Happen?" *The Denver Post*, April 25, 1999, Section H, p. 1.

3. John Drescher, *If I Were Starting My Family Again* (Intercourse, PA: Good Books, 1994), n.p.

4. Laura Schlessinger as quoted by Ross Werland, "Should You Spy on Your Teen?" *Reader's Digest*, July 2000, p. 160.

5. Kathi Kemper, M.D., "ADHD, or Another Problem?" Available: http://onhealth.com/ch1/columnist/item,35494.asp, March 15, 2000.

6. Joan Hansen, "Chess Champ Takes on Newhart's Best," *Saddleback Valley News*, March 15, 2000, p. 3.

7. Kathi Kemper, M.D., "ADHD Changes Begin at Home," Available: http://onhealth.com/ch1/columnist/item,35504.asp, January 2, 1999.

8. Theresa Walker, "Parents vs. Peers," *The Orange County Register*, September 15, 1998, Accent, p. 1.

9. Used by permission of Family First, Inc., Tampa, FL.

10. Carolyn Poirot, "Sudden Mood Swings Called Clues to Abuse," *Fort Worth Star-Telegram*, October 28, 1984 as quoted by Zig Zigler in *Raising Positive Kids in a Negative World* (New York: Balentine Books, 1996), p. 184.

11. Zigler, p. 191.

12. From the author's book *Tomorrow Starts Today*, October 14 selection, used by permission of Barbour Publishers, Uhrichville, Ohio, 1999.

13. Ibid., February 24 selection, used by permission of Barbour Publishers, Uhrichville, Ohio, 1999.

14. Ibid., February 25 selection, used by permission of Barbour Publishers, Uhrichville, Ohio, 1999.

15. Ron Stodghill II, "Where'd You Learn That?" *Time*, June 15, 1998, Vol. #151, No. 23., pp. 52-60.

16. Ibid.

17. Available: http://hlthed.sask.com/cni/units/10.4.2/tbsui_103.html, November 16, 2000.

18. Sharrel Keyes, "To Choose to Live—Why Suicide Is Not for Me," *His*, January 1980, p. 7.